The Spanish-Speaking World

A practical introduction to sociolinguistic issues

- Clare Mar-Molinero

First published 1997
by Routledge
11 New Fetter Lane, London EC4P 4EE

Simultaneously published in the USA and
Canada
by Routledge
29 West 35th Street, New York, NY 10001

Typeset in Sabon, Futura, Times and Optima
by Keystroke, Jacaranda Lodge,
Wolverhampton
Printed and bound in Great Britain by
TJ International Ltd, Padstow, Cornwall

*British Library Cataloguing in Publication
Data*
A catalogue record for this book is available
from the British Library

*Library of Congress Cataloguing in
Publication Data*
Mar-Molinero, Clare, 1948–
    The Spanish-Speaking world : a practical
introduction to sociolinguistic issues /
Clare Mar-Molinero.
    – (Routledge language in society : 3)
Includes bibliographical references and
index.
    1. Spanish language—Social aspect.
    2. Sociolinguistics.
I. Title. II. Series.
PC4074.75.M38 1997
306.4'4'0943—dc20   96–43952

ISBN 0–415–12982–6 (hbk)
ISBN 0–415–12983–4 (pbk)

Contents

Part one

THE POSITION OF SPANISH IN THE WORLD

Part two

EXPLORING LINGUISTIC VARIATION

Part three

CURRENT ISSUES: LANGUAGE AS NATIONAL IDENTITY MARKER

Illustrations

Maps

Tables

Acknowledgements

I would like to thank Rodney Ball and Patrick Stevenson, my co-editors for this new series, for our useful brainstorming sessions and for sharing the pressure as deadlines loomed. I am especially grateful to Jane Freeland for the detailed and encouraging comments that she gave me on an earlier draft.

Material for parts of the book, in particular for Chapters 1, 3, 9 and 10, appear in an earlier and much more condensed form in Mar-Molinero and Smith (1996): Chapter 4.

Thanks are due to the following publishers who have granted permission for the use of certain extracts, the full sources of which are listed in the Bibliography: the Spanish Ministerio de Educación y Ciencias, Editorial Gredos, Editorial Ariel for the extract from Salvador (1987), Teresa Timsley, Cambridge University Press for the extract from Batchelor and Pountain (1992), Earthscan Publications, Centro de Investigaciones Sociológicas, Sage Publications for Table 5.2, Mouton de Gruyter on behalf of the *International Journal of the Sociology of Language*, Prensa Española on behalf of ABC, Addison Wesley Longman for the extract from Holmes (1992), Oxford University Press for the extract from Romaine (1994), Bilingual Press/Editorial Bilingüe, Arizona State University for Table 21 (Carlos A. Solé) and pp. 132–133 (John M. Lipski) from *Sociolinguistics of the Spanish-Speaking World: Iberia, Latin America, United States* (1991), edited by Carlos A. Klee, *El País* for five newspaper articles, Ediciones Paidós Ibérica for the extract from Meseguer (1994), Ediciones Akal for the extract from *Política linguística y sentido común*, Thomas Nelson and Sons Ltd for the extracts from Hickey (1977) and *La Vanguardia* for the article by Josep Miró i Ardèvol published in *La Vanguardia* 22 May 1991.

Every effort has been made to obtain copyright permission for all the extracts that have been reproduced here. The author and publishers would be grateful to hear from any copyright holders they were unable to contact.

Introduction

T HE AIM OF THIS BOOK is to offer students the opportunity to explore for themselves a wide range of sociolinguistic issues in relation to the Spanish language. It is intended principally for undergraduate students of Spanish who have a reasonably advanced knowledge of the language, but who may have little or no knowledge of linguistics in general or sociolinguistics in particular. Relevant theoretical concepts are introduced where necessary, but the emphasis throughout is on encouraging readers to think for themselves and to tackle specific problems. To this end, each chapter is punctuated with a series of practical tasks and discussion questions designed to stimulate readers to pursue issues raised in the text in greater depth, and concludes with suggestions for further reading.

The book has been written with a typical semester-length course in mind, and it could therefore be worked through as the principal course text. However, although there is a progression within each chapter and through the three parts, it is hoped that the structure of the book is sufficiently flexible to allow it to be used in various ways to suit particular needs. For example, individual parts or chapters could be selected to complement other material,

and students or tutors can decide for themselves which tasks to attempt. The tasks are graded in terms of difficulty and the time required to tackle them.

Coverage is inevitably a problem with a book of this size, as it would be impossible to deal comprehensively with all the geographical regions where Spanish is spoken. More detailed coverage is given to Spain, the birthplace of the Spanish language. However, wherever possible examples are given from different parts of Latin America, although to pretend to cover the linguistic configuration of over twenty nations is outside the scope of a book of this nature. Throughout there is an attempt to present a representative 'flavour' of Latin American Spanish. In particular, students are encouraged to pursue their interests in Latin America through the tasks set and the further reading lists.

The structure of the book

Part one aims to give the reader an overview of the position of Spanish in the world, including a historical introduction to its development and expansion, a discussion of its geographic range, and an examination of its status and role *vis-à-vis* other languages with which it comes into contact. The tasks include both small-scale activities, such as working on definitions of important concepts as well as more wide-ranging reflective exercises such as essays, projects or dissertations.

Part two is the most practical part of the book. The aim here is to encourage readers to explore social and regional variation in Spanish from a 'micro-sociolinguistic' perspective. The focus shifts from the role of the language as a whole to the forms and functions of individual features. This involves, for example, looking at ways of identifying distinctive features of regional speech forms, analysing similarities and differences between written and spoken Spanish, investigating the 'social meaning' underlying different forms of address, and exploring the sociolinguistic implications of the gender system in Spanish. There are many practical tasks and exercises involving the analysis of written texts and transcripts of speech, and there are opportunities to carry out small-scale 'empirical' work, such as conducting questionnaires or gathering material for analysis.

Part three pulls together issues which emerge in the first two parts and which hold a particular current interest. These reflect the specific questions of the moment in areas where Spanish is spoken. By this stage, readers should be in a position to employ the tools and skills they have acquired from the earlier chapters to analyse these issues. For this reason, the tasks here are normally based on readings from primary texts, such as newspaper articles or legal documents.

This book is not intended as an introduction to sociolinguistics *per se*. Where concepts and terminology are used that might be new to readers, they are either briefly explained in the text or used as the basis of tasks requiring readers to find out (or work out) for themselves what the terms mean. The key concepts are given in bold, the first time they appear in the text, and they are listed in a selective 'index of terms' at the end of the book to provide a quick source of reference and act as an *aide-mémoire*. However, the whole purpose of the book is to demonstrate that there are few, if any, hard and fast answers to sociolinguistic questions and to encourage readers to think for themselves and reach their own conclusions.

How to use this book

Each chapter includes a series of tasks and discussion questions, which are interspersed through the text rather than being listed separately at the end. The purpose of this is to encourage readers to pause and reflect on the issues as they go along and to give them the opportunity to pursue particular topics in greater depth.

It is assumed that readers will have access to an academic library and many of the tasks can only be tackled by making use of the resources normally found there. Readers will only get the most out of the book if they actively seek information and ideas from a wide range of sources (for example, textbooks, journals, newspapers, maps, television and radio, CD-ROMs, the Internet). Most of the tasks should be feasible in this way, but a few may require contact with native speakers of Spanish, and one or two may best be tackled during a period of residence in a Spanish-speaking country. To help readers decide which tasks to attempt, they have been graded in terms of difficulty and/or the time and resources required:

■ a question or task that invites the reader to reflect briefly on a particular point before continuing;

■■ a question or task that involves a practical activity (such as writing a list of ideas, or reformulating a text), or requires the reader to do some further reading in order to explore a particular issue in greater depth or to gather necessary information etc.;

■■■ a question or task that gives the reader the opportunity to undertake an extensive study of a particular issue, for example in the form of an empirical project or an essay or dissertation.

The 'Further reading' section at the end of each chapter is intended to direct readers towards suitable material on specific topics raised in the chapter. The books and articles listed here are referred to by their author and their date of publication; full details of each reference are given in the Bibliography at the end of the book. The following are recommended, however, as general information about sociolinguistic and linguistic issues, and should be useful background reading for all the main topics of each chapter.

Introductory reading

Crystal, D. (1987) *The Cambridge Encyclopedia of Language*, Cambridge: Cambridge University Press.

Fasold, R. (1984) *The Sociolinguistics of Society*, Oxford: Blackwell.

Holmes, J. (1992) *An Introduction to Sociolinguistics*, London and New York: Longman.

Wardhaugh, R. (1992) *An Introduction to Sociolinguistics*, Oxford: Blackwell.

• • •

The position
of Spanish
in the world

Part one

Chapter 1

The origins of Spanish
The historical context
of a dominant language

Introduction

Spanish is spoken today by over 350 million people. For the vast majority of these people Spanish is their mother tongue. From the Iberian Peninsula, where Spanish first developed, the language has been exported across many continents and established as the national language of many countries. Colonisation and imperialism, however, were the reasons for this dramatic spread, and the legacy of this enforced dominance can still be seen in many of the places where Spanish is spoken. Even in the Iberian Peninsula itself the status of Spanish is not unproblematic as it continues to coexist, sometimes uneasily, with those minority languages that still survive on the peripheries of the Peninsula. The history up to the present day of these minority languages will be specifically examined in Chapters 3 and 10. In Latin America, too, Spanish is often in conflict with the pre-colonial indigenous languages, as will be seen in Chapter 2.

Part one will trace the history of the development and expansion of Spanish, or Castilian as it is now interchangeably known, showing how and where its relationship with other languages leads to tensions. This chapter will look at the origins of Spanish, and how it emerged in the Iberian Peninsula and developed as the dominant language of that region.

■■ Before continuing any further, think about the development of Western European countries in general, and how far they have emerged as unified states from fragmented communities and medieval kingdoms. Waves of conquests, particularly significant being the Roman one, have influenced the development of linguistic varieties. How typical do you think this pattern was in the evolution of language in Spain?

What makes Spain's linguistic history different from many of its neighbours', is the conquest and long occupation of large parts of the Peninsula by the Arabic-speaking Moors. The bringing together of potentially hostile groups across the Peninsula during the *Reconquista* against this common enemy helped create a unity and establish a pecking order which was to prove very important to Spain's early nation-building.

From Latin to Castilian

Except for Basque, all the languages we associate today with the Iberian Peninsula are derived from Latin and form part of the **Romance languages** continuum.

- ■■ What other languages are part of this continuum? Deciding how to demarcate these different languages presents important questions of definitions: what is a dialect and what is a language? Fasold (1984) and Edwards (1985) will help you in your answers. Can you think of ways of defining these terms which make sense of how we now divide up the various Romance languages?

- ■■ Nowadays we usually talk of the existence of five discrete languages in the Iberian Peninsula: Castilian, Portuguese, Catalan, Galician and Basque. Discuss the concept of a 'discrete' language. What, in your view, characterises separate languages in this sense? As you read the rest of this chapter, decide what have been the principal factors which have allowed these five to survive as languages, and not others, such as, for example, Aragonese or Asturian?

During the Roman occupation, the cultured language of writing and political power was still Classical Latin. However, the spoken language was what is normally called Vulgar Latin. Over time the various local populations created new forms of this which we could call separate **vernaculars**. These developed from a mixture of the previous local languages and Vulgar Latin and reflected their diverse geographical and environmental contexts. The fragmentation of the declining Roman Empire saw a corresponding fragmentation in the various forms of Latin-based languages being used. By around the eighth century, five distinct language groups all derived from Latin had emerged on the Peninsula: Galaico-Portuguese, Asturian-Leonese, Castilian, Aragonese and Catalan. At first Castilian was the least evolved of the post-Roman Empire forms of Vulgar Latin. It retained, therefore, marked differences from spoken Latin.

In 711 the Moors invaded the Iberian Peninsula and although they remained for very little time in the more northern and western parts, their final expulsion only took place seven centuries later. Castile was particularly prominent in the opposition to the Moorish invaders, which, in turn, led Castilians to a new, and never-to-be-lost, position of importance during the centuries of the *Reconquista*. Castile came to dominate the Peninsula, culminating with the marriage of the Catholic Monarchs, Ferdinand and Isabella, in 1469 and the final ousting of the Moors with the fall of Granada in 1492. This dominance inevitably gave status to the Castilian language, which was increasingly used, even in non-Castilian territories, as the language of culture and administration. A standard form of Castilian had emerged, in particular as the result of efforts by the Castilian king Alfonso X in the mid-thirteenth century to standardise the written language.

■■   The concept of **standard language** will be referred to throughout this book. Try to find out a little more about what this concept refers to (see, for example, Edwards 1985, Wardaugh 1992 or Romaine 1994).

Coinciding with the Catholic Monarchs' and Castile's political domination, the first standard Spanish (i.e. Castilian) grammar was produced by Antonio de Nebrija in 1492.

■   Yet another highly significant event around this same date, 1492, was the birth of Spain's American empire. Consider why this event might also have favoured the rise of Castile's dominant role in Spain, especially given the fact that the Catalans and Galicians were forbidden from trading with the New World colonies.

The end of the fifteenth century, then, for most commentators marks the birth of modern Spain. This period heralds the beginning of the creation of a Castilian hegemony, a hegemony born out of solidarity in the face of the common Moorish enemy, throughout the newly formed state, and, with it, the repression of the minority communities along the peripheries.

■■   Define and discuss the concept of **hegemony**.

Spanish nation-building and Castilian linguistic supremacy go hand-in-hand, but, nonetheless, they do not succeed in entirely eliminating non-Castilian communities.

■■   Consider the importance of language as a marker of national identity. To do this you will need to discuss terms such as 'nation' and 'state' and decide how far communities are grouped naturally through shared characteristics and how far they are forced into being by political and/or military organisations (see Edwards 1985 and Wardaugh 1987).

Through wars and the politics of royal marriages the various kingdoms of the Peninsula were brought together, albeit still very loosely. However, attempts to include Portugal in this were not successful. Portugal was established as a separate kingdom in 1134, and only briefly reverted to Castilian dominance under Philip II from 1580–1640, thereafter remaining a separate state from Spain.

Initially the so-called 'unification' of Spain created first by the Catholic Monarchs' marriage and finally by the annexation in 1512 of Navarra, was a very loose concept, hardly akin to our present notion of 'nation-state'. This is reflected too in the range of languages still in use across the Peninsula, despite the dominance of Castilian. Its political superiority, as the language of the court and government and the expanding empire, was mirrored too during this period by a flourishing literary output in Castilian which became known as Spain's Golden Age, and was marked by the work of authors such as Cervantes, Lope de Vega, Calderón, Góngora and Quevedo.

The establishment of a 'national' language

It is really not until the seventeenth century, as Spain began to abandon her more ambitious empire-building and started to look more inwards on herself, that moves to consolidate Spanish national identity took shape which directly influenced language policies.

■   Consider why the following secret memorandum written by Conde Duque de Olivares in 1624 to the King is so important in this process:

> The most important thing in Your Majesty's Monarchy is for you to become king of Spain, by this I mean, Sir, that Your Majesty should not be content with being king of Portugal, of Aragon, of Valencia, and count of Barcelona, but should secretly plan and work to reduce these kingdoms of which Spain is composed to the style and laws of Castile, with no difference whatsoever.
>
> (quoted in Linz 1973: 43)

Clearly a major obstacle to any such centralising policy, and to a sense of Spanish, not merely Castilian, identity, would be the existence of different vernaculars (linked with their diverse regional identities) thus bringing the need for one 'national' language onto the agenda.

■■ What do you think is the significance of calling the language 'Spanish' (*español*) or 'Castilian' (*castellano*)? Discuss this issue in the context of all the areas where the language is spoken (see, for example, Alvar 1986: Chapter 3). Do these terms have a different meaning when used by English speakers?

On the death of Charles II in 1700 there ensued a bloody conflict over the succession. The losing pretender (Archduke Charles) was backed by, amongst others, many of the communities where non-Castilian languages were still widely spoken, such as Aragon, Catalonia, Valencia and Mallorca. Partly, then, as a result of their defence of the defeated Archduke, a heightened repression of non-Castilian languages followed, with moves to impose Castilian throughout Spain in administration and the law. The successful claimant, Philip V, was the first of the Spanish Bourbon kings, who further extended a tight centralised political system, along the lines of the model being developed then in France, from where he came. As a result of their and their pretender's defeat the Catalans and others had their last residual local laws and privileges revoked. This accelerated a programme of massive Castilianisation of their institutions and public life.

During the eighteenth century two issues in particular play a significant role in furthering the position of Castilian throughout Spain. These are the increasing use of Castilian by the Catholic Church, and the use of Castilian in the education system. To this also can be added the effect of universal male conscription into a Castilian-speaking army. As power became centralised in Madrid, so too did the appointment of bishops, with the result that Castilian-speaking bishops were now commonplace in the non-Castilian speaking areas. While the lower clergy often resisted this loss of the use of the mother tongue, the Church had an important influence in extending the use of Castilian, both in its ecclesiastic duties and its education services. In 1768 Charles III decreed that 'throughout the kingdom the Castilian language be used in administration and in education' (quoted by Siguan 1993: 25).

■■ In what ways is education so important in helping to create national identity (see, also, Chapter 11)? In particular remember that with the arrival of the printed word, written educational materials became more widespread. What are these materials and how can they reflect national issues?

In the eighteenth and nineteenth centuries education became increasingly accessible and, eventually, compulsory. The claims that it was necessary to learn Castilian in order to have access to the political administration or to the language of culture were, in reality, secondary to the basic desire by the monarchy and government to give children a particular Spanish way of being which was essentially that of a Castilian identity.

A further factor contributing to the consolidation of the prestige of Castilian as the national language was the establishment of the Royal Academy of the Spanish language in 1713.

■■ What does the Academy's motto *'limpia, fija, y da esplendor'* tell us about its role in promoting the Spanish language? Compare this to other language academies in such places as France or Italy (see, for example, Edwards 1985). Does the absence of such language academies in Britain and the USA demonstrate a different role for language in their nation-building?

In 1808 Spain, like so much of Europe, was invaded by Napoleon. As had occurred previously during the *Reconquista*, this had the effect of uniting even those who had previously been in conflict with the central government with a sense of solidarity against the common enemy. It seemed that, for the first time, a sense of Spanish (rather than Castilian, Catalan, Galician, etc.) patriotism was experienced. However this was followed by a century of deep divisions and internal conflict, which failed to build on that moment of national patriotism. During this period, language issues seemed to take something of a back seat at national level. On the one hand, the Liberals, the Federalists and, much later, the left-wing supporters of working class groups, all viewed the 'national' language as an enabling vehicle to empower people in political decision-making, and thus feared the divisive nature of promoting regional languages over Castilian. On the other hand, and surprisingly, the traditionalist Carlists, based in rural and often non-Castilian speaking regions of northern Spain, did not appear to pay any attention to issues of local languages.

■■ Try to find out more about nineteenth-century Spain and its crisis in nation-building in order to answer why the different sides in constant conflict paid so little attention to the role of regional languages. (You will find useful information on this in Mar-Molinero and Smith 1996.)

Despite this lack of interest from the main political actors in the centre, however, the latter half of the nineteenth century saw the resurgence of cultural activities in languages other than Castilian in various parts of the Peninsula, notably in Catalonia, Galicia and the Basque Country (see Chapter 3). These cultural movements signalled new or increased literary outputs, which led to a focus on the written language for the first time in many centuries. This period, then, also saw significant work in the **standardisation** of the language in the areas of **codification** and **elaboration** of the non-Castilian languages, that is to say, with the production of dictionaries, grammars and standard orthographies. (Chapter 10 discusses further the role of this kind of activity as part of language planning.)

It needs stressing that whilst Castilian had by now dominated all walks of public life in Spain and was clearly the national language, the other languages were still spoken, to a greater or lesser extent, by their communities. Although they had not disappeared altogether, in many areas they were in a classic diglossic situation *vis-à-vis* Castilian.

■■ The concept of **diglossia** is widely used to discuss sociolinguistic situations, and many commentators use it when talking about the different linguistic varieties of Spain. Diglossic situations are said to occur when two linguistic varieties or separate languages coexist but perform different and identifiable functions in the speech community. The terms 'High' and 'Low' varieties are used to describe these types of functions. The former refers to public and formal uses, such as the language of the administration, the law, and often education and the media, whereas the latter refers to more private, informal and intimate language use (see, for example, Romaine 1994: 45–48).

Make sure you discuss and understand this term. Be aware of its limitations as a definition of sociolinguistic situations. For instance, we will see later that it is not always easy to divide the use of, for example, Catalan and Castilian into separate, ring-fenced functions. Speakers tend to be in fact far more fluid and flexible in their language use. Any rigid separation, it could be argued, is produced by political dictates rather than naturally occurring usage.

Language in twentieth-century Spain

As Spain entered the twentieth century its sense of national identity was challenged on the one hand by the lingering reaction to the final loss of a diminished empire (in 1898) and with it a loss of international prestige, exacerbated by an inability to modernise, and, on the other, by the impatience from the linguistic minority communities on the periphery towards the imposition of the central state bureaucracy and its administrative incompetence. Spain's political instability throughout the crises of the nineteenth century had prevented her from joining the modernising and industrialising processes experienced by other European nations. While the imperialist past and Bourbon centralism had ensured Castilian dominance, creating a nation-state similar to others in Europe, the chaotic political situation of the nineteenth century had failed to bring the linguistic minorities entirely to heel, allowing peripheral nationalisms to flower in a climate of cultural nationalism inspired by European-wide **Romanticism**.

■■ Do you know of any other European Romantic movement, for example in Germany or France or Britain? Try to find out some more about this movement and what it stood for.

This, then, is the legacy that Spain brought into the twentieth century, and which is largely to blame for the consequent decades of repressive centralist dictatorship in this century.

The beginning of this century saw Spain in a very volatile situation, with a traditional, conservative and highly centralised political system which desperately needed to modernise its economy and build up its industries to compete with the rest of Western Europe. The tensions in the regions reflected this economic and social instability, heightened by the newly rediscovered cultural awareness of their different identities. The history of this period reflects these uncertainties with waves of social unrest, particularly in Catalonia, as well as a certain prosperity and liberalising of the social and political structures during the First World War, when neutral Spain benefitted as a provider to the warring factions, a process which allowed a certain increase in Spanish industrialisation. This was followed, as economic recession set in, by a period of military dictatorship (Primo de Rivera 1923–31) which reinforced the centralist nature of the regime. However, in 1932 the abdication of the King and the proclamation of a Republic (the Second Republic 1932–36) gave Spain a few years of enormous political and social change, much of which has been replicated since the death of Franco. During this short period the regional languages were given some recognised status which challenged, to a small extent, the position of Castilian as the national language.

It was the forces of centralism that won the bitter 1936–39 Civil War, and therefore the years that followed saw harsh repression by the Franco dictatorship of the minorities on Spain's periphery. During this regime the language question was a highly political topic.

■■ It has become apparent in this chapter how closely the development of language, especially the national language, is linked with political events and regimes. Can you think of other examples of highly centralised regimes or dictatorships where language has been an important element in characterising its society? In what kind of ways do you think the Franco regime would have wanted to influence language use and why?

The use of minority (non-Castilian) languages was seen as anti-patriotic. These languages were therefore proscribed from public use and ridiculed. A situation, once again, of enforced diglossia existed in regions such as Catalonia, shutting down the expansion in the use of minority languages which had taken place during the Republic. The regime carefully chose to refer to these languages as 'dialects' of Spanish (with the exception of Basque). It was claimed that the non-Castilian languages were inferior, and they were characterised as the speech only of the uneducated and peasantry.

In the early part of the Franco period infringements of the laws prohibiting the use of languages other than Castilian were heavily punished with fines and imprisonments. But in 1966 the dictatorship relaxed its attitudes a little with the passing of the so-called Freedom of Expression Law, which removed the stricter forms of censorship in favour of prior, self-censorship. As a result, private organisations were now allowed to teach mother-tongue languages other than Castilian, and publishing in these was once more permitted. To some extent this reflects the confidence of the Franco regime, as it judged that it had little to fear from unflattering views published in non-Castilian languages, given the inevitably limited readership.

■ The regime deliberately encouraged a certain type of media coverage in non-Castilian languages, such as reports on dance competitions or local fiestas or how to cook local dishes, leaving serious news and politics to be reported in Castilian. Why do you think it did this?

This policy of apparent tolerance, based on the belief that the non-Castilian languages were perceived as inferior and more trivial, was given something of an unexpected knock in the late sixties by the emergence of a highly successful and influential Catalan folk music movement, known as the *Nova Cançó*. Mirroring such protest movements in other parts of the world, notably the anti-Vietnam protest singers in the USA, these musicians wrote and performed in Catalan and achieved large followings in terms of their record sales and attendance at their concerts. These concerts became focal points for protest against the Franco regime and were often either banned or broken up. The boost this movement gave to the prestige of Catalan and to a wider recognition of it as a means of mass communication was very important in its revival.

Franco died in 1975. Since his death Spain has seen dramatic changes and reforms. The implications of these for language use, and for the position of Castilian, will be analysed in detail in Part three.

■ ■ Having read this chapter, now construct a table which shows each of the important historical periods discussed, and list next to them any significant events in terms of the language issues. Include at least: the Roman Empire, the Moorish invasion, the *Reconquista*, 1492, the seventeenth century, the eighteenth century, the nineteenth century and the twentieth century.

Further reading

For introductions to the history of the Spanish language, see Díez, Morales and Sabín (1977); Lapesa (1980), which is a little out-dated but still authoritative; Penny (1991), a very accessible introduction in English. For an introduction to the history of Spain and Spanish nation-building, see Linz (1973); Carr (1982); and Mar-Molinero and Smith (1996). There are good overview chapters in Fasold (1984) and Edwards (1985) on the basic concepts concerning language and nationalism.

•   •   •

Chapter 2

Spanish in Latin America

THE PART THAT SPANISH has played in the construction of the national identity of the nations of Latin America is somewhat different from that which we have traced in the Iberian Peninsula. Here, as the language of the colonisers, Spanish cannot claim a 'natural' right to be the national language. Despite this, it is, nonetheless, the national and/or official language of the majority of Latin American nations.

Spanish is spoken by a significant part of the population in Mexico; in the Central American states of Guatemala, Honduras, El Salvador, Nicaragua, Costa Rica and Panama; on the Caribbean islands of Cuba, the Dominican Republic and Puerto Rico (whose special status will be discussed in Chapter 12); and in the South American states of Colombia, Venezuela, Paraguay, Uruguay, Argentina, Chile, Bolivia, Peru and Ecuador (see Map 2.1). In some cases this involves the large majority of the population, in others the significance lies in the fact that it is the language of the elites.

Under the Spanish Empire these eighteen now independent states formed part of far larger political groupings, being divided into four Viceroyalties, and were not considered separate discrete nations. They were conceived by the Spaniards as part of a greater imperial *Hispanidad*, but had in fact brought together indigenous empires and ethnic communities whose borders were different again from those of the colonial or the post-colonial periods.

■■ Compare the way nation-states emerged in Europe – from medieval kingdoms, isolated communities and sprawling empires – with the political map created by Spanish colonisation in the Americas. Notice again how artificial political borders usually are, and the extent to which they do not necessarily align with cultural and ethnic groups, or with linguistic demarcation. This mismatch will often lead to the need for enforced groupings, both political and linguistic.

The emergence of separate states in Latin America during the wars of independence in the early nineteenth century involved the need to construct separate national identities for these countries. Spanish played an ambiguous role in this nation-building, representing as it did the language

MEXICO

México

La Habana

CUBA

DOMINICAN REPUBLIC

PUERTO RICO

GUATEMALA
Guatemala
San Salvador
EL SALVADOR
HONDURAS
Tegucigalpa
Managua
NICARAGUA
COSTA RICA
San José
Panamá
PANAMA

Caracas

Bogotá

COLOMBIA

VENEZUELA

Quito
ECUADOR

PERU

Lima

La Paz

BOLIVIA

Brasilia

PARAGUAY

Asunción

Santiago

URUGUAY

Buenos Aires

Montevideo

CHILE

ARGENTINA

TIERRA DEL FUEGO

MAP 2.1   Spanish-speaking nations of Central and South America

of the former coloniser and of unity rather than diversity. However, insofar as the elites of white European descent were simply importing Europeanised culture and concepts of society, the fact that a European language should be the language of government and the state was never in real doubt. This language was of course Spanish.

In most Latin American states, to a greater or lesser degree, there exist indigenous **Amerindian** languages, which are still widely used as well as Spanish.

■■ This term is used to describe the many native American languages which had existed for centuries before the arrival of the Europeans. What factors do you think contributed to keeping these languages separate and distinct from each other? Consider the geography and size of Latin America. Compare the impact of Spanish on this region with similar conquests in other areas, such as the legacy of Latin brought with the Roman Empire.

At the time of the arrival of the Spaniards, hierarchies between these languages also existed, creating the status of **lingua franca** for some of these, such as Quechua of the Inca Empire, or Nahuatl of the Aztec Empire.

■■■ Find out what a lingua franca is from any good introductory socio-linguistics book (for example, Fasold 1984; Appel and Muysken 1987; Wardaugh 1992). Discuss other examples. It might be argued that such languages emerge because of the need for wide communication and contact. Why do you think that this has not had the result of gradually eradicating all linguistic difference across the world as people feel the need to talk to each other? One essential function of language is of course to communicate. But why do we also stick to using separate languages which are mutually unintelligible? When you have considered this, you can find further discussion on the symbolic value of a language to its community of speakers, i.e. language as an identity marker as well as a means of human exchange, in Fasold (1984) and Edwards (1985).

The presence of large groups speaking these pre-colonial languages is still significant today in the Andean states, parts of the Amazonian basin, most of the Central American states, and Mexico. These groups consist, in their great majority, of underprivileged, second-class citizens of the state within which they live. In other Latin American states, such as Cuba, the original indigenous populations have been all but wiped out.

These are not, however, the only influences in the modern Latin American linguistic context. At least three other features need to be taken into account. The first is the extent to which other, non-Spanish immigrant languages have left their mark, such as the Italian speakers in Argentina; various tight-knit German speaking communities (for example, in Paraguay or Venezuela); the groups of Spanish immigrants who in fact brought their own non-Castilian language with them, such as Galician, Basque or Catalan; and the more recent arrival from the Far East of speakers of Japanese, Chinese or other Asian languages. To some extent these groups have influenced the form of Spanish that they have been integrated with, particularly as far as lexical and phonological features are concerned.

■■   Find examples of such communities (Lipski 1994 is a helpful source). For example, there is a large Welsh-speaking community in Patagonia, in southern Argentina.

The fortunes of languages are so bound up with their environments that it is of interest to observe how a language will fare differently when exported away from its original homeland. So not only is the development beyond Spain of Spanish, a widely spoken language, important to study, but, from a sociolinguistic point of view, it is also interesting to observe how a small language, like for example Welsh, a threatened minority language in its own birthplace, survives in an entirely new context.

More widely spoken languages like German and Italian have also had an influence in Latin America. Argentinians have come to use the Italian word *che* to such an extent as to find themselves given this nickname, which, of course, was the case with the well-known Argentinian revolutionary, 'Che' Guevara, whose name was really Ernesto.

Another important factor which has influenced the language situation in Latin America is the large influx of African-born slaves during the years of the Empire, and in some cases, beyond. Again, not all Latin American states have been permanently influenced by this group in terms of language, although most show their influence in terms of race and culture. Only in the areas where these populations were most highly concentrated, such as the Caribbean and parts of the Atlantic coast of Central America, has the phenomenon of **pidgin** and **creole** languages developed by the slaves left its mark.

■■■ The Caribbean is an important area to observe pidgin and creole varieties, although these are more dominant in French- and English-speaking former colonies than Spanish. Find definitions and explanations of the meanings of 'pidgin' and 'creole' (see, for example, Appel and Muysken 1987: Chapter 15; Romaine 1994: 162–191). How would you account for considerably less occurrence of Spanish-based creoles in this region? (For further reading, see Lipski 1994.)

In present-day Latin America a further factor, English, has influenced the variety of Spanish spoken – not only English as a world language which is dominating all parts of the world in terms of economic power and technological advancement, but more particularly, the English of the USA because of the very dominating and overbearing influence the USA has on its less developed southern neighbours. However, in the nineteenth century it was the British who controlled much of the economic power in Latin America (building railways and owning mines and large stretches of agricultural land), making English a status symbol amongst the ruling classes. An illustrative example of this influence is the British-Argentine community, well-documented by Yolanda Russinovich Solé.

> The economic self-determination of the British language group in Argentina gave it sociocultural self-determination as well. Viewing themselves as economic colonizers, they opted for segregation, establishing their own schools, clubs, churches, neighbourhoods, press, and hospital . . . Rooted in Great Britain's political, cultural, literary, and economic attainments of the past – their ideas and ideals were easily sustained by the Empire's primacy in their very own present.
>
> (Solé 1995: 114–115)

■■■ Investigate and compare this cultural and social isolation practised by the elites of the British imperial class with the behaviour of the Spaniards or the French when settling in colonial lands. Discuss how this might affect language use.

But now it is not only the elites of Latin American states who are exposed to (above all US) English; in urban areas its use in the media (especially television and advertising) bring even the poorest into contact with it.

The Castilianisation of Latin America

The language policies of the Spanish Empire ensured the inevitability of the **Castilianisation** process despite the huge and inaccessible territory and large non-Castilian speaking populations. These policies were to a large extent influenced by the role of religion in the colonising of Latin America. Initially the Spanish missionaries saw the sense in learning native languages and teaching Christianity to the natives through them. Up until the time of their expulsion from Latin America in 1767 the Jesuits, in particular, were solid defenders of the language and culture of the indigenous population. However, the original imperial decrees that priests should learn the indigenous languages lapsed by default as these people preferred to use native interpreters, a group who were also widely used by the Spanish administrators of the colonies. As time went by, too, the colonisers saw the importance of Castilianising the local native nobility and thereby gradually assimilating them to European ways. It is not however until the seventeenth and eighteenth centuries when the use of Spanish and a thorough Castilianisation of the conquered peoples became the official Spanish policy.

■ Before reading any further, what do you think are some of the reasons for this?

Colonising powers usually seek to impose their language, their culture and their dominance, but given that the official excuse for colonisation was the Catholicising crusade, it was also often claimed that only Spanish, rather than an indigenous language, was capable of transmitting the ideas and concepts of Christianity. The idea that languages can be plotted hierarchically in terms of their suitability, value, and so on is one disclaimed nowadays by most linguists, who argue that a language will always have the potential to respond to any given context. (This 'communicative competence' of a language to react appropriately in any given social context will be discussed in detail in Chapter 6.) In earlier centuries, however, the notion of a linguistic hierarchy – with European languages at the top – was commonplace. A reason particular to Spain, also, was the increasing goal, especially of the Bourbon Spanish kings of the eighteenth century, to centralise and hegemonise all things Spanish by the dominance of Castile.

■ Compare this with the Castilianisation process taking place then in Spain itself (see Chapter 1). It was not only the clergy in remote parts of Latin America who were instructed to use Castilian, but also those in, for example, Catalonia.

Part of the official language policy of Castilianisation was to set up schools in rural areas to educate the indigenous population through Spanish. These schools seldom materialised, however, partly through lack of resources, partly because the local elites were not keen on the captive workforce being educated. The few schools which were established were run either by the Church or more enlightened *encomenderos* ('land-owners'). The use, therefore, of local languages continued much as before, while Spanish became firmly entrenched as the language of government, the Church, high culture and the dominating classes. Bilingualism of course did start to develop, both as the result of racial intermixing and the Indians' need for survival. One critical difference, also, between Spanish and the indigenous languages was the fact that Spanish had a highly developed written form, making wider communications quicker. The role of literacy and its ambiguous status for the Latin American indigenous population remains a dilemma today, which will be examined more fully in Chapter 11.

All of the former colonies by the time of their independence used Spanish as their dominant language. In the drafting and re-drafting of national constitutions over the following century, many of these republics would see the need to recognise Spanish as their national or official language, thereby giving it importance in the formulation of national identity. Today ten of the Latin American states that were former Spanish colonies enshrine in a current constitution the status of Spanish or Castilian.

- The majority of these refer to Spanish as the 'official' language, but in some states Spanish is referred to in legal decrees as the 'national' language. Clearly in such manifestly multi-ethnic societies the distinction between these two terms is extremely important. How would you distinguish between the two terms? Is this a similar distinction as that which we can make between 'state' and 'nation'?

In some of those states where 'national' is used, such as Paraguay, Ecuador and Peru, the term is now used to refer to indigenous languages as well.

Constitutions, it can be argued, form part of the national consciousness by enshrining rights and duties of a nation's members, but they also establish citizenship, and these rights and duties are only accessible if citizenship can be attained and understood. Those members of a state who do not speak the official language are in danger of being disenfranchised; and those who do not read the legal documents issued in this language may well be considered second-class citizens, if citizens at all. In very many of the original constitutions of the early nineteenth century, citizenship and its associated rights were limited to those who could read and write. With the realisation that the states could not or would not deliver the necessary education to allow substantial parts of their populations to reach this goal, the constitutions were gradually amended. The implications of this for literacy and bilingual education programmes even today will be discussed later.

■■ Peru and Paraguay are two particularly interesting examples of the importance of language to their national identity and how this is reflected in their constitutions. As you read this summary of the two, however, notice the extent to which they are refreshing examples of the awareness of linguistic identity, but at the same time by no means flawless models.

Paraguay

The status of languages in the Paraguayan constitutions has always reflected the very different situation of the main indigenous language in this former Spanish colony compared with all the other Latin American ones. Largely as a result of the fact that this was where the Jesuits had their headquarters until they were forced to leave the Americas, Guaraní enjoyed and has continued to enjoy a prestige and acceptance that no other pre-colonial language has known. Even amongst the creole class and in the urban areas, there are few, even today, who are totally monolingual in Spanish alone. Guaraní enjoys a special place as the language of Paraguayanness, even while Spanish is the language of government and official public use. 'Guaraní is . . . a prerequisite for status as a genuine Paraguayan' (Fasold 1984: 15). The social stigma attached to using and learning other indigenous languages has not occurred with Guaraní. The Castilianisation process was not so strong here. However, even here, Spanish is predominantly the language of the education system, despite recent attempts to introduce Guaraní in bilingual programmes at the earliest stages of schooling. It is also important to note that the dominant status of Guaraní has not led to a wider tolerance and acceptance of indigenous languages in general in Paraguay, where small communities of other pre-colonial languages suffer a similar fate to most such languages in Latin America. What seems at first sight a model situation in terms of the legal status of an indigenous language, on closer examination reveals ambiguities.

Peru

Recently in Peru, too, legislation has attempted to upgrade the major non-Spanish languages spoken there. First, in 1975, Quechua was proclaimed a co-official national language. But the failure of the radical military administration of 1968–75 to impose changes in favour of the indigenous populations on the nation as a whole (partly because of international pressures against radical reforms) meant that this legislation was replaced in 1980 by a law which gave co-official status with Spanish to Quechua or Aymara in designated regions. The limiting of language rights to particular areas is questionable, restricting languages, as it does, to confined and often insignificant areas (see further discussion of the relation of language and territory in Chapter 10). In the case of Peru this language legislation denies the very important existence of Quechua and Aymara in the urban areas, and in particular, Lima, to which much of the indigenous population has been forced to migrate.

In the main, nonetheless, language policies of post-colonial Latin American states can be said to have shaped societies where increasingly mono-lingualism amongst indigenous speakers has given way to bilingualism or monolingualism in Spanish only. The reasons for this reflect the aware-ness on the part of these states of the need to create a sense of national unity in states which were, on the whole, multi-ethnic, or, put another way, composed of many nations. Besides being the language of public administration, education, religion and so on, Spanish also served as a lingua franca in commercial transactions between indigenous groups with different, non-Spanish languages. Increasingly, therefore, it was seen as the language of economic survival and of social mobility. Monolingualism in an indigenous language, on the other hand, confirmed dispossession and under-privilege.

Spanish in twentieth-century Latin America

By the twentieth century, then, it could be said that Spanish had become a factor in creating national identity, often imposed as a form of national unifier. However, communities which did not have Spanish as their mother tongue were very often the largest groups in their respective state (for example, in Peru, Bolivia and Guatemala).

■ Consider what the description of 'minority group' means here, as it clearly does not refer to population size.

The pressure to learn and use Spanish throughout the former Spanish colonies has increased even more strongly throughout the twentieth century. The typical consequences of modernisation, slow though it has been to come to many parts of Latin America, is the main explanation. Internationalised economic markets, advanced technological media and communications and, especially, migration to urban areas have led to an increase in the need to learn Spanish. As development and modernisation produce major social changes, the ensuing marginalisation of large sections of Latin America's poor (often non-mother-tongue speakers of Spanish) needs to be addressed through education and literacy programmes.

■■ However, these same programmes raise difficult questions about identity, and particularly national identity for those whose native culture is very different from the Westernised culture of most Latin American states' elites. Can you think what some of these issues are?

The desire and need to be part of the political system around them, even where this may mean adopting certain culturally foreign ways, has become an imperative for many of Latin America's dispossessed indigenous people. Bilingual education programmes which allow for proper parallel treatment of both languages and cultures are clearly an ideal objective that could help to satisfy the need both to have access to the wider political, economic and social processes through the knowledge of Spanish, and to maintain the indigenous mother tongue and cultural assumptions. Examples of good practice in this respect are few and far between and instead provision has tended to be made simply for assimilationist programmes aimed at transferring the learner at the earliest stage from his or her mother tongue to a monolingual programme in Spanish. (See Chapter 11 for further discussion of language and education in Latin America.)

Spanish as a world language

As economic, cultural and technological exchanges are increasingly performed beyond national frontiers, so too are linguistic demarcations, as can be seen with the expansion and domination of English as a world language.

■■ What do you think constitutes a 'world language'? How does this differ from 'lingua franca'? One feature of a world language is the quantity of second-language speakers of the given variety. Does this fact mean that Spanish, which is predominantly spoken by first-language speakers, is not truly a world language? Are we really looking at economic and cultural influence rather than simply population size of a linguistic community when we talk about world languages? Compare Spanish in this sense with other possible world languages like French and Japanese.

Spanish, as we have seen, has only ever been partially tied down to specific national identities in Latin America. There have been attempts by some states to distinguish their Spanish from that of other Latin American nations and to emphasise it as an identity marker, such as in Mexico. Indeed, many of the Latin American states have their own Language Academies (loosely linked to Spain's Royal Academy). Certainly, different identifying accents and vocabulary uses have developed in the various Latin American states, but neither these nor the Spanish of Spain have ceased to be manifestly recognisable and comprehensible as part of one and the same language (see Chapter 4).

This shared language has led to moves to create a supra-national identity of pan-*Hispanidad* amongst Spanish speakers, through such organisations as the Comunidad Iberoamericana de Naciones, a potential counterweight to the economic and cultural influence of the USA, or to the emerging European Union. Such supra-national alliances seek homogeneity and serve to emphasise transnational similarities, which in Latin America are above all the legacy of European colonisers: their political and economic values, religion, culture and, of course, their language. (See Part three, also, for further discussion of the spread of Spanish globally.)

Further reading

For a very useful overview of the language situation in Latin America, see Lipski (1994). A good range of sociolinguistic issues in Latin America is discussed in Klee and Ramón-García (1991). For an introduction to the history of Latin America concentrating in particular on the period of the wars of independence from Spain, see Lynch (1973) and, for a more general overview, Bethell (1995).

•   •   •

Chapter 3

The other languages
of Spain

Chapter 3

V ERY FEW COUNTRIES contain within their borders a homogenous population speaking the one national language.

■ Which countries can you think of where this might in fact be true? In the nineteenth century in particular, many European states tried to claim that this was the case, which led to the persecution of many minority languages. A quick glance across the map, even of Europe, soon demonstrates this to be untrue. How many languages are spoken by sizeable groups in Britain, or in France?

Whilst it is true to say that most countries contain significant parts of their populations who speak different languages, one legacy from the desire to create monolingual nation-states, particularly in nineteenth-century Europe, has been the reality that the majority of the populations of these states are monolingual in the dominant national language. Beyond Europe in particular, however, the phenomenon of multilingualism is extremely common, if not the norm.

■■ Discuss the consequences of multilingualism. We have already briefly touched on the concept of diglossia, which may or may not be a stable situation. Frequently language contact leads to very unstable situations wherever languages are in conflict, reflecting tensions within the communities. Many situations can result from languages operating in the same space and the same community. What do you think the following terms represent and can you think of examples of each: **language shift**, **language death**, **language revival**? (For further reading about these, see, for example, Wardaugh 1987.)

As we have already seen, Spanish comes into contact with other languages in all the areas where it is spoken as a major language. In this chapter we will concentrate on the situation of those languages which have survived in Spain despite the dominance of Castilian. We will be asking to what extent these minority languages have suffered from contact with Castilian. Has there been language death, shift or revival? The current position of these languages, since the death of Franco, will be discussed more fully in Part three. Here we will provide a historical framework of the contemporary situation, emphasising the significance of the minority languages as a thorn in the flesh for Castilian as flagbearer of Spanish national identity.

We have seen in Chapter 1 that the four linguistic varieties normally accepted as the separate languages of Spain since unification as one country are Castilian, Catalan, Galician and Basque. The first three are all Romance languages, and their similarities are of significance to us, in the same way that Basque's total difference is also relevant. As part of a fluid language continuum we are faced with a problem of demarcation of boundaries (linguistic and geographic). Inevitably there are other linguistic

MAP 3.1 Modern Spain, highlighting Galicia, El País Vasco and Cataluña

varieties spoken in Spain which have reasons to claim to be separate languages, but which are usually subsumed under one of the four mentioned above. For this reason the discussion below will focus on the three minority languages, Catalan, Galician and Basque, but will make reference to some of the other varieties linked with them.

■   What do you see as being the potential pitfalls of this decision to concentrate on just these three languages when discussing the position of minority linguistic groups in Spain?

Catalan

At its peak, Catalan was the principal language of a large area, including not only present-day Catalonia itself, but also parts of Southern France, Aragon, Valencia, the Balearic Islands, as well as enclaves in Italy, North Africa and Greece. Its prestige during this period (eleventh to fourteenth centuries) was on a par with French and Italian, as well as other languages of the Peninsula like Castilian and Portuguese. It increasingly replaced Latin (and later Provençal) as the language of cultural and literary production. Only in Aragon did it remain merely the spoken variety. Literary and philosophical output flourished, and even while Catalan's political power diminished in the fifteenth century to be replaced by Castilian dominance, Catalan could still boast a Golden Age in letters, notably in Valencia. From the sixteenth century onwards with the rise in Castile's power that we have noted, Catalan was on the decline, and parts of the original *Països Catalans* (Catalan countries) were lost (as Roussillon to France). Repressive laws and the increased presence of a Castilian-speaking hierarchy meant Catalan lost its prestige and became largely a spoken language only.

■■   Consider the importance of this move away from the use of the written language. Writing down a language produces a standardising tendency. Norms must be chosen, prescribed and adhered to. With the loss of this function, language use becomes more disparate, producing more and more varieties and dialects. This phenomenon can potentially cause a language eventually to disappear altogether, although this did not of course occur with Catalan. Is the presence of a written form the only way we can guarantee the survival of a language, particularly nowadays?

The process of Castilianisation and official persecution of the Catalan language continued to marginalise Catalan until the counter efforts in the nineteenth century and the movement known as the *Renaixença*. This movement is usually considered to take its first inspiration from poetry-based activities. However, the main thrust of the *Renaixença* took place during the second half of the nineteenth century and around the turn of this century, and became far more than a cultural expression, inspiring also a political movement. Certainly the *Renaixença* was initially dominated by important literary output, which reflected the influence of the European Romantic movement, as writers exalted their past and also particularly highlighted (even mythologised) forgotten groups and traditional cultures with their popular legends and stories. In Catalonia this encouraged writers to express their literature in their mother tongue which had barely been used as a cultured literary language for two or three centuries. The Catalans achieved an impressive output of lyric poetry and extended this interest to the popular domain with such activities as the *Jocs Florals* which were oral poetry competitions, modelled on the lines of similar medieval contests, and later taken up in the Basque Country and Galicia. These played a similar role to the eisteddfod in Wales, which also experienced a major revival in the early nineteenth century.

Heightened cultural awareness, however, led Catalans to want to emphasise and control their separate identity in a way that the centralised governments of the Spanish state did not allow. This, of course, included the promotion of their own language, particularly through literature and other cultural activities and through the education system. In particular in the many periods of central government crises of the nineteenth century, Catalans felt frustrated by the Spanish state. From these experiences emerged regionalist and eventually Catalan nationalist aspirations, which, however, were preceded by a Spanish-wide Federalist movement. The nineteenth-century Federalists were inspired by such Europeans as Proudhon, but were in the main Catalans, albeit Catalans originally operating at national (Madrid) level, the most significant being Pi i Margall. But by the second half of the century and as self-awareness among the Catalan urban bourgeoisie increased, this federalism took on a more strictly Catalan tone. An increasing desire to protect and modernise their local industry in the midst of the traditional and largely agrarian Spanish state pushed the Catalans towards redefining their sense of identity politically as well as culturally.

Throughout the intellectual development of the ideas of the *Renaixença*, language emerges as the central issue around which the

Catalans based their claims to a separate identity, and which was also established as a central plank in their political debates. This is a theme taken up by the leading politician of the *Renaixença*, Enric Prat de la Riba. For Prat de la Riba, language, along with culture and territory, formed the spirit that defines the nation. Prat de la Riba founded the Catalan bourgeois nationalist party, the Lliga, and in 1914 its electoral success meant he became the president of the Catalan Mancomunitat which was a first step in the direction of enhanced local government for Catalonia. The latter did not have many powers, particularly compared with its later successor, the Generalitat of the Second Republic and today, but it continued to promote the Catalan language, setting up the Institut d'Estudis Catalans under whose auspices much codification and elaboration of the Catalan language (such as the production of dictionaries, orthographies and grammars) was carried out by the Catalan linguist Pompeu Fabra.

■■ Why do you think Catalan nationalism and particularly the Catalan language experienced this resurgence at precisely the time it did? When thinking about this, you need to take into account events Europe-wide. The nineteenth century saw an expansion of nationalistic awareness, of Romanticism, and of modernisation and industrialisation. Catalonia has always been the most industrialised economy of Spain's regions. Why might this fact be relevant to its dealings with the national government in Madrid? How might this affect language issues?

As regards the rest of the former Catalan-speaking areas of the Peninsula, that is Valencia and the Balearic Islands, the cultural revival of Catalan did have some impact but none in terms of political expression. Whereas in Catalonia the Catalan language had always retained its prestige even with the upper classes, in Valencia, by the nineteenth century it was only a low-status language spoken by the rural lower classes. An environment in which to produce literary output was, therefore, considerably less developed, but some writers in Valencia did publish in Catalan, and moves to define the Valencian variety, as separate from Catalan, also took place at this time. Politically, though, Valencia shared the predominantly agrarian character of the rest of Spain – while not, perhaps, the country's backwardness as Valencia's agricultural export market was expanding very successfully. But her links with Spain-wide tendencies, usually liberal, were stronger than any interest in separation or identification with the Catalans.

In the Balearic Islands too there was some revival in terms of literary output in the Catalan of the Islands, but, in this very conservative rural area, there were no political moves away from the central state. An important event for the standardisation of Catalan, begun at this time, was the elaboration of a dictionary of Catalan–Balearic–Valencian varieties by the Mallorcan Antoni Alcover.

Basque

The Basques were forced to retreat further and further into the more inhospitable, and therefore less accessible, of their lands by the constant wars which mapped out the Peninsula from Roman times to the sixteenth century. Despite these conflicts with invading forces, the Basque language has been only a little influenced by external linguistic groups. In return for retaining their cherished *fueros* (rights), the Basques accepted Castilian, and eventually Spanish dominance more readily than the Catalans, and were thus able to maintain a separate but subordinate identity. The Basque language continued to be spoken in much the same way as Catalan, as an oral variety in a diglossic situation, Castilian being the language of power. Unlike the Catalans they did not have a significant medieval literary, written corpus in Basque to serve as a basis for maintaining the unity of the language. Far more than Catalan or, in its turn Galician, Basque has suffered from divisions into dialects and subdialects, some almost mutually incomprehensible. To some extent this also reflects the geographical terrain, with many isolated mountain and valley settlements where contact was minimal. This dialectal fragmentation of the language has been an obstacle right up until the present day. Politically, too, the Basques were divided, with no one strong kingdom, as the Catalans had. The communities in Viscaya and Guipuzcoa had no one leader, and were rigidly separate from the Kingdom of Navarre. Still today Navarre is only partially Basque-speaking.

■■ Consider the extent to which a language flourishes because it has a tight geographical focus, a centre for its cultural as well as popular expression. For the Catalans this has always been Barcelona. What correlation do you think there might be between the strength of a language and a readily identifiable centre (or centres) of cultural focus?

As in Catalonia, the nineteenth century saw an increased awareness of Basque culture and eventually a form of Basque nationalism; as in Catalonia, too, the Basque Country, unlike the rest of Spain, experienced major industrial and economic development parallel with other parts of nineteenth-century Europe. But besides these similarities, there are very many differences between the two regions, as their different histories already suggest. The two most obvious differences between the modern nationalisms that developed in the two regions are, first, the role that language played in constructing their identity, and, second, the very different reactions by the industrial bourgeoisie in the two regions. The contrasting levels of popular involvement in the two regional movements are also significant, with the Basque nationalist case being backed only by a very small group of committed intellectuals.

While in Catalonia it could be argued that the cultural and political nationalist movements grew out of the industrialisation process taking place there, in the Basque Country almost the opposite is the case. The Basque urban bourgeoisie was content to work with Madrid, and in fact the major Spanish banking elites were Basque ones, intricately bound in with the Spanish state's economy and political fortunes. The Basque language was barely spoken in urban areas, or by the middle class, and while it was indeed middle-class intellectuals who wished to revive the Basque identity, they had to rely on the 'pure' Basques of the isolated rural areas as their base.

In both Catalonia and in Galicia, cultural revivals preceded political expressions of regional identity. In the Basque Country it was largely a radical political manifesto which, along with cultural representation, inspired Basque nationalism at the turn of the century. The father of modern Basque nationalism was Sabino Arana (1865–1903). He and his followers saw Basque urban society with its modernising industrialisation and influxes of immigration as threatening the essence of Basque identity, which he set out to re-confirm and define. Unlike the Catalan case, it was unrealistic here to place too much importance on the role of language, as Basque was not a widely-spoken language, even compared with Catalan or Galician. In fact, in the nationalist context, it was only emphasised as a way of excluding those who were clearly not Basque by birth or descent. In this early nationalist thinking the most important common value for the Basques was race. This emphasis on race ('blood' and 'origin') contrasts significantly with Prat de la Riba writing at the same time about Catalan nationalism, where the emphasis is above all on the bonding effect of language. The choice of race and not language as the prime core value in

Basque nationalism marks a significant difference from Catalonia, and one that characterises the two regions' nationalisms in the twentieth century also.

■■ Consider this concept of 'core value' as a way of defining group identity. Race and language are obviously two of these, what other values can you name? What would you consider the core value of English or German or French identity? Do you think language can be a core value for any of the Latin American nations' identities?

Since the use of the Basque language was less widespread, and with little in the way of a literary tradition, it is not surprising that the literary cultural movement in the Basque Country was on a far smaller and less wide-reaching scale than its Catalan counterpart. The nationalist movement, however, did focus its political aspirations through the Partido Nacionalista Vasco (PNV), founded and led by Arana, which shared many similarities with Prat de la Riba's Lliga.

The Basque nationalists have always regarded Navarre as part of the Basque Country (in the same way as they claim the three French Basque provinces). However, Navarre has in fact been politically separate from the Basque Country for many centuries, the Kingdom of Navarre being the last such to be annexed by the Crown of Castile in 1512. Like the Basques, Navarre enjoyed her own special local laws, *fueros*, but unlike the Basques these remained in place even under Franco. Since a part of the Navarrese population has always been Basque-speaking, particularly in some of the provinces in the Pyrenees, there has existed an uneasy relationship towards Basque nationalism with a partial recognition of some shared culture and language and some support for Basque nationalist parties. Even today Navarre recognises this linguistic situation in its present Statute of Autonomy.

Galician

As has already been seen, the earlier form of the language spoken in Galicia was Galaico-Portuguese, a romance variety that emerged from the Roman occupation, which came later to this part of the Peninsula than to any other. Claims that Galician and therefore Portuguese were strongly influenced by the Celtic languages spoken in this area until the arrival of the Romans are hard to substantiate, although they do play a significant part in the construction of Galician identity and beliefs. It is generally considered that the separation of Galician from Portuguese took place around the eleventh century, although this was a very slow and gradual process, and both languages claim a share in the success of Galician lyrical poetry which was widely acclaimed in the Middle Ages (twelfth to fourteenth centuries). Santiago de Compostela's importance as a pilgrimage destination meant that this literary production was known further afield than the Iberian Peninsula and was in turn influenced by the Provençal troubadours. The Castilian king Alfonso X was known to have written in Galician, reflecting the high regard for Galician letters during this period.

The historical-political reasons behind the separation of Galicia and Portugal have left their mark too on the linguistic outcomes. As the kingdom of Portugal was established from the beginning of the twelfth century, a national language for all state purposes evolved. The Galaico-Portuguese variety that was spoken there underwent major influences distinct from the Mozarabic spoken in the southern areas that the Portuguese kings annexed. This move southwards also changed the focal centre of the new kingdom to Lisbon, and away from the influence of Galicia. As Portuguese blossomed and developed as the national language of an important empire, Galician shrank into an oral form only, increasingly dominated by Castilian. Castile's political domination of Galicia and over the Galician language was even greater than that over Catalan, partly because there was a less strong written tradition to build on (the lyrical poetry was essentially an oral genre), and because Galicia did not enjoy such a political power base as the Catalans. The early adoption of Castilian by the Church in a region where religion was so important also brought about the virtual demise of Galician.

The nineteenth-century cultural revival in Galicia, her *Rexordimento*, differs significantly from those which took place in Catalonia and the Basque Country in that it was restricted to literary and cultural production. The political awareness which followed these movements in the other two regions was much slower to emerge in Galicia, and we can only really talk of a political articulation of Galician nationalism from the twentieth century. The principal explanation for this is the economic condition of nineteenth-century Galicia, which was an extremely poor agricultural society, suffering high levels of emigration to other parts of Spain, Europe, and above all, Latin America. Galicia was a backward and traditional society not experiencing the challenges of modernisation or industrialisation that were taking place in Catalonia and the Basque Country. It was also geographically very isolated, a feature that has always helped shape Galician history.

Nonetheless European-wide influences such as Romanticism did lead Galician intellectuals to examine their historical and cultural roots and rediscover pride in their region and language. Some important writing was produced in Galician (although, again, mostly poetry). *Xogos Florais* were held, modelled on the Catalan ones, and the poetry read at these was published. The most famous writer of this movement is Rosalía de Castro, who, however, reverted to publishing only in Castilian towards the end of her life. By the turn of the century a Galician Royal Academy had been established with the aim of standardising and codifying Galician. The need to decide on norms for the written language and to represent Galician identity was important not only, as in the other regions, to overcome the great variety of existing dialects, but, particularly, in the case of Galician, to separate it clearly from Portuguese. This latter relationship continues to present a dilemma in present-day Galicia (as we will see in Chapter 10).

Linguistic frontiers are never rigorous, but, rather, blurred areas along a continuum, and therefore it is no surprise to discover important Galician-speaking communities beyond the political confines of Galicia, particularly in western Asturias. This has been an important factor in the explanation of why the Asturian-Leonese language did not develop as strongly as its early history might have suggested. Squeezed by the emerging Castilian on the one hand and by the then robust Galician-Portuguese varieties on the other, Asturian-Leonese never emerged as a linguistic rival. Claims for a discrete language in this area do still exist today, but the stronger influence of Galician, as well, of course, as the dominance of Castilian, have helped prevent these varieties from taking any significant hold.

■■ From the above discussion (and see, also, Siguan 1992), draw up a list summarising the main features which contribute to the separate identities of the Catalans, the Basques and the Galicians, noticing those that all three have in common and also where they differ from each other. It is a mistake often made to lump all three communities together as 'Spain's linguistic minorities' without due respect and understanding of their differences. Do you think that this is in general a danger that we risk when making statements about linguistic minorities and their relationships with other groups? Should we only treat each group case by case?

Further reading

There is good coverage of the histories of the non-Castilian minority languages in Díez, Morales and Sabín (1977). The most up-to-date and fully comprehensive discussion of the minority language communities in Spain can be found in Siguan (1992). For a thorough discussion of the effects and consequences of multilingualism, see Edwards (1994).

•   •   •

Part two

Exploring
linguistic variation

Chapter 4

Regional and social variations in Spanish

As WE SAW IN CHAPTER 1, the Spanish language that we know today originated from Castilian, the dominant variety to emerge during the *Reconquista* and as the Spanish nation took shape. Besides its essentially Latin base, this variety had been influenced by Arabic as a result of the long Moorish occupation of parts of the Iberian Peninsula.

In Chapter 1 attention was drawn to the need to have a working distinction between 'language' and 'dialect'. Along the Romance continuum we can mark off languages and also dialects. Sometimes it is hard to know where to place the borders. As we have already seen, political considerations often determine whether something is referred to as a 'language' or 'a dialect'. Such considerations have to take into account the size of the population who speaks the variety. They involve asking such questions as: does this community have a separate political and economic identity; or is this variety standardised and has it a written form? When the answers to most of these questions are 'no' and the community is a small one then we are more likely to refer to this variety as a dialect. A further feature often associated with dialects is their position in a hierarchical structure, of which some parent 'language' is the head. Under this language may exist various dialects which are more or less mutually intelligible to all the speakers of this family hierarchy.

Different dialects have always been associated with different regional contexts, and, increasingly, are recognised as frequently denoting social differences. Whilst the most immediately obvious feature of a dialect to hit us is its **phonological** characteristics – the 'accent' – dialects are characterised by other linguistic variation such as **morphological**, **syntactical**, and, particularly, **lexical** features.

■ Before examining Spanish dialects, think about your own mother tongue. Can you think of examples of dialects across English (or whichever is your first language)? In particular, think of different grammatical structures, different vocabulary, as well as the diverse accents.

Obviously over the centuries diverse dialects of Spanish have developed. Nonetheless, as with most languages, there is an accepted 'standard' dialect which is largely seen as the norm for more educated and professional activities, as well as being taken as a standard for what is or is not perceived as 'correct' Spanish.

■■ What factors make one dialect the standard dialect rather than others? Compare standard English, or standard French with standard Spanish. Where did the former two dialects originate from? (See, for example, Crowley 1989 and Grillo 1989.)

Dialects in Spain

Standard Spanish, or Castilian, originated from central-northern Spain and is associated with the variety spoken in the area including Toledo (from where it probably originated), Madrid and Burgos. This form of Castilian has been reinforced from early on by being the variety spoken in various prestigious centres of learning such as Salamanca, Alcalá de Henares and Valladolid. It is often called the Burgos-Castilian dialect. Significantly, its roots coincide with the seat of government (Toledo was the first capital of united Spain, and then Madrid), but it was not without some rivalry from Seville and the southern Spanish variety.

■ Thinking about the historical context traced in Chapters 1 and 2, why would Seville be an important competitor to the dominance of the central Castilian dialect?

Whilst being aware of the dangers of over-generalised conclusions, it could be argued that these two dialects – the Burgos-Castilian and the Sevillian – are the foundations for the basic differences between the present-day Spanish of Spain and the Spanish of Latin America. Both were of course then influenced by a wide range of specific factors, the consequences of geography, history, climate, demographic movements, and so on. In the case of Spain, Castilian came into contact with the other major languages on the periphery, which affected the variety of Spanish then spoken in these areas. As we have seen, the Amerindian languages and the languages of non-Spanish-speaking immigrants influenced the different dialects to emerge in Latin America.

While emphasising that dialectal borders are very fluid and are always shifting, we can divide the present map of Spain into six main dialectal regions (not including those areas where the three designated separate languages are spoken). Besides Castilian, these are: Asturian-Leonese, Aragonese, Andalusian, Extremaduran and Murcian (see Map 4.1).

As might be expected, the main features of *Asturian-Leonese* are those that bring it close to Galician and Portuguese, in particular the accent, with the diphthongising of clear Castilian vowels: *primeiro* for *primero* or *roubar* for *robar*. Some words retain the initial 'f' as in the original Latin instead of the 'h' of modern Castilian: *farina* (*harina*) or *facer* (*hacer*).

Aragonese, on the other hand, shows influences both from Leonese on one of its borders (and therefore indirectly Galician-Portuguese) and from Catalan on its eastern border. It too has signs of diphthongisation and the use of 'f' for 'h', with a significant quantity of Catalan words entering the Aragonese vocabulary. This dialect is also characterised by the use of subject pronouns after prepositions, such as *con yo*, or *para tú*, and for its *-ico* diminutive ending.

Andalusian is one of the most distinctive of the Spanish dialects, partly because of the use of the *seseo*.

■ What do you think *seseo* refers to? Its opposite, the *ceceo*, is probably the characteristic most commonly associated with the sound of Spanish by non-Spanish speakers, often satirised as an English lisp.

A far greater proportion of native Spanish speakers pronounce the 's' and 'z' as a *seseo* than as a *ceceo*. However, it is significant that this feature of standard Castilian dialect, the *ceceo*, is associated by non-Spanish speakers across the world with Spanish, despite it being the mark of only a minority of Spanish speakers. This seems to confirm the prestige that standard forms have in the eyes not only of their own speech community but beyond it.

Other features of Andalusian Spanish, many shared also with Extremaduran, are a weakening of unaccentuated vowels, the loss of 's' or 'r' at the end of words (but the lengthening of the preceding vowel), the aspirated initial vowels, and the virtual disappearance of the 's' in the middle of a word. Another feature of much of Andalusian Spanish is the use of *Ustedes* instead of *Vosotros* for the informal as well as the formal plural.

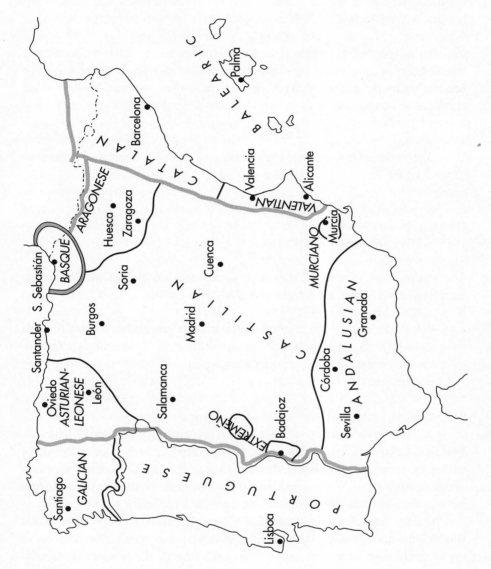

MAP 4.1 Languages and dialects of Spain

Source: Based on Díez, Morales and Sabín 1977: 104

47

These regional differences, it must be stressed, are greatly affected by social influences. Therefore, the rural Andalusian farm labourer or working class migrant now living in Barcelona will have a far more emphasised form of the dialect than a professional educated Andalusian, such as the former Prime Minister, Felipe González, who comes from Seville. However, whilst social class is important in determining the way Spaniards speak, most Spaniards, whatever their social class, who do not come from the area where Burgos-Castilian is spoken as the dialect of origin, will have some regional marking in their speech. (See Chapter 5 for more discussion of the status of Spanish accents.)

■ Compare this fact to the situation in Britain. Do we expect those occupying high-prestige professional jobs to display a regional accent?

Spanish dialects in Latin America

There is still a tendency in Latin America to consider the standard Burgos-Castilian dialect as the prestige dialect even whilst it varies so much from the variety of Spanish spoken in all Latin American countries. The existence of an organisation of language academies from all these nations linking them with the Real Academia Española contributes in part to this, as it helps maintain the sense of an ultimate norm. However, in fact there is a huge diversity of Latin American dialects, all of which vary appreciably from the standard Spanish of Spain. These differences exist at all levels, phonological, morphological, syntactic and lexical.

As we have already mentioned, it is usually considered that the Andalusian dialect, and particularly that of Seville, had a major influence on Latin American Spanish varieties. While it has probably been an exaggeration to say this was because most Spanish colonisers came from Andalusia, it is true that a significant number did. Seville was the heart of the organisations and preparations for the voyages to the New World, and this in turn gave prestige to its linguistic variety amongst those embarking on emigration to the Americas. The importance of the Canary Islands as a major stopping point on the voyage over is also significant, as a substantial proportion of future settlers also came from these islands. The Canary form of Spanish shares many characteristics in common with Andalusian, and therefore would leave a similar legacy.

Today the different dialects of Latin American Spanish are at least as diverse as the twenty nations where Spanish is spoken. In the development of these dialects we should notice that those areas with the strongest links with Spain for trading and administrative purposes, particularly Mexico City and Lima, retained during the days of the Empire the closest forms to peninsular Spanish, with the peripheral regions diverging the most noticeably. The presence of the Spaniards in Cuba until the end of the nineteenth century has also left the variety of Spanish spoken there with marked lexical similarities to peninsular dialects (whilst developing its own distinctive accent). Areas which received concentrations of Spanish immigration, even after independence, also maintained stronger linguistic links.

It would be a mistake to over-emphasise the influence on Spanish of the native Amerindian languages. The influence at the level of lexical items, particularly the naming of objects new to Europeans such as *chocolate*, *tomate*, *canoa*, *tabaco*, and so on is important, but the low esteem accorded to the indigenous populations meant that there was only limited influence from these conquered communities on the lives and speech habits of the colonisers.

Whilst students of Spanish are familiar with the many different accents heard throughout Latin America, the wide variety both compared with Spain and between Latin American nations in terms of lexical differences is sometimes less expected.

■■ How much of the following 'test' of Spanish words and expressions can you get right? As you check the 'soluciones', notice how there is often more than one possible answer, underlying the differences between the varieties of Spanish across Latin America.

ENRIQUEZCA SU 'GUACHINANGO'

Un pequeño ejercicio para conocer su dominio del léxico hispanoamericano

Escoja la acepción que corresponde, en su concepto, a cada vocablo.

1   *Pololear*: A) Regar las flores. B) Conseguir novio o novia. C) Solicitar empleo. D) Enojarse.
2   *Guagua*: A) Bebida de maíz fermentado. B) Niño de brazos. C) Autobús. D) Armadillo.
3   *Mamar gallo*: A) Tomar el pelo. B) Consumir bebidas no alcohólicas

en una fiesta. C) Asistir a un sepelio. D) Conquistar a una mujer.

4   *Guindar*: A) Golpear. B) Comer frutas directamente de la mata. C) Peinarse con bucles. D) Colgar.

5   *Tecolote*: A) Caballo. B) Rasquiña. C) Cacto venenoso. D) Lechuza.

6   *Guayabo*: A) Ratón. B) Perseguidora. C) Resaca. D) Cruda.

7   *Pavoso*: A) Relativo al peligro. B) Relativo a la mala suerte. C) Relativo a las aves de corral. D) Relativo a la siembra.

8   *Barrilete*: A) Asiento doble. B) Florero de madera. C) Cometa. D) Puñal.

9   *Respajilar*: A) Ahuyentar. B) Mezclar el naipe. C) Insistir. D) Despertarse.

10   *Yapa*: A) Un animal. B) Regalo que se agrega a una compra. C) Enfermedad de las llamas. D) Pan de mandioca.

11   *Quilombo*: A) Prostíbulo. B) Medida de la sal. C) Pestaña. D) Pequeña cabaña sin paredes.

12   *Corotos*: A) Bártulos, trastos. B) Pereza, aburrimiento. C) Gusanos. D) Aves de rapiña, buitres.

13   *Huera*: A) Máquina para moler la caña de azúcar. B) Delgada. C) Alta. D) Rubia.

14   *Machado*: A) Candado de doble llave. B) Profesor. C) Borracho. D) Reja alta.

15   *Birome*: A) Artefacto para escribir. B) Estrábico. C) Hombre que se disfraza de mujer. D) Miedo.

16   *Pela*: A) Zurra, azotaina. B) Yegua, hembra del caballo. C) Persona baja, pequeña. D) Mujer pública, ramera.

17   *Escuincle*: A) Cabro. B) Chino. C) Niño. D) Gurí.

18   *Patilla*: A) Arruga en el rostro. B) Discusión. C) Sandía. D) Monja que no viste hábito.

19   *Panela*: A) Ventana pequeña. B) Producto sólido del jugo de caña de azúcar. C) Recipiente cubierto en que se colocan las viandas. D) Adivina, pitonisa.

20   *Palta*: A) Alfombra rústica. B) Aguacate. C) Maíz molido. D) Hamaca.

Soluciones

1)   B: *Pololear*: Conseguir novio o novia (Chile).
2)   B y C: *Guagua*: En Cuba, autobús; en Chile, niño de brazos.
3)   A: *Mamar gallo*: En Colombia, Venezuela y otros países, tomar del pelo.

4) D: *Guindar*: Colgar, en Guatemala y casi todo el Caribe.
5) D: *Tecolote*: Búho, lechuza, en México.
6) A, B, C, y D: *Guayabo*: Es, en Colombia, lo que «ratón» en Venezuela, «perseguidora» en Perú, «resaca» en otros países y «cruda» en México.
7) B: *Pavoso*: Que trae mala suerte, en Venezuela.
8) C: *Barrilete*: Cometa, en Nicaragua y otros países.
9) A: *Respajilar*: Ahuyentar, echar de un sitio a alguien, en República Dominicana.
10) B: *Yapa*: Regalo u obsequio que se da al comprador; se escribe también *ñapa* y se emplea en casi toda Suramérica.
11) A: *Quilombo*: Prostíbulo, en Paraguay, Argentina y, en general, el Cono Sur de América.
12) A: *Corotos*: En Panamá y otros países del área Caribe, bártulos, baratijas, trastos.
13) D: *Huera*: que tiene el cabello rubio, en México.
14) C: *Machado*: En Bolivia, borracho.
15) A: *Birome*: Bolígrafo, en Argentina.
16) A: *Pela*: Zurra, azotaina, paliza, en Costa Rica y otros países.
17) A, B, C y D: *Escuincle*: Al niño se le llama «cabro» en Chile, «chino» en Colombia, «gurí» en Argentina y «escuincle» en México.
18) C: *Patilla*: Sandía, en Puerto Rico y otros países.
19) B: *Panela*: Bloque que se fabrica luego de hervir el jugo de la caña de azúcar, en Ecuador y otros países.
20) B: *Palta*: En Chile, aguacate.

(based on an article in *Cambio 16* 23.V.88)

In Latin America, as elsewhere, social factors are as important as regional ones in influencing dialects. The gulf between the privileged few and the under-privileged masses in Latin America means that the social dialect differences are very noticeable and reflect the inequality of educational provision and limited access to more widely used standard forms. There is no single Latin American standard dialect, as such, although as we have already noted there are those who will maintain that the standard is in fact the Burgos-Castilian dialect. Instead, what tends to occur is that the prestige dialect of each country is that of the capital city. In this sense the national variety is confirming its role as nation-builder. Sometimes a speaker will aspire to the dialect of a distant metropolis although he or she actually shares a dialect with adjacent communities on the other side of a political border, who attribute to this dialect a high prestige status.

The study of social dialects

Over the years the study of dialects has been an important part of historical and descriptive linguistics. The creation of linguistic atlases was often the end result. There have been many of these carried out both in Latin America and in Spain. However, this type of linguistic description was limited in achieving a reliable and generalisable picture of Spanish dialects.

■ These studies often took small isolated rustic communities. In what way would this be limiting? What is the typical composition of small rural communities?

In an increasingly predominantly urban society these studies have failed to give us useful exploitable models of what is happening to Spanish.

■■ An urban example: Bilbao

The study of linguistic features of the residents of Bilbao is a good example of the range of variables that need to be considered. The relatively stable town community up until the late nineteenth and the early twentieth century has now been significantly changed by:

(a) major industrialisation;
(b) influx from the immediate countryside around the city;
(c) influx from other parts of the Basque Country generally attracted by work and a better economic situation;
(d) immigration from other parts of Spain;
(e) the revival of the use of the Basque language;
(f) greater provision of social and cultural services as part of the city's general infrastructure;
(g) improved education provision to a wider range of the population;
(h) a wider range of skilled jobs;
(i) greater exposure to media, publicity, etc.

Speculate in what ways these factors might affect the linguistic habits of the population of Bilbao which will shape the characteristics of their dialect. How do you think this situation would differ from a small rural community, such as, for example, in the area round San Sebastian.

More recently studies have been made in urban areas (e.g. Havana, Mexico City, Caracas, Buenos Aires, Santiago de Chile and Bogotá in Latin America) which have been able to capture the many influences that help create dialects in modern-day life.

The difference in the focuses of the rural as opposed to the urban studies is essentially that of *regional* dialects versus *social*. However, there is some overlap in both: clearly rural dialects, whilst mostly concentrating on the regional features, have a greater tendency to represent poorer, less educated and less mobile populations; on the other hand, urban dialects, at the same time as they reflect social class, economic environment and so on may also be typical of given geographical areas. The extent to which the identification of the speakers' regional and/or social origin affects attitudes to the use and prestige of different linguistic varieties will be discussed in Chapter 5.

In an attempt to understand why people speak the way they do and what are the influences contributing to their particular dialect, socio-linguists have increasingly used the method of identifying **social networks** as a way of mapping dialects. If we accept that we are highly influenced in our speech behaviour by those with whom we interact, we can study social dialect variation by identifying people's networks of contact and communication: with whom do we mix in the family context, socially, at work and through contact such as our children's schools? What becomes of great interest is to discover the extent to which this portrays a homogeneous picture or an altogether more complex one. Are those people with whom we come into contact daily at work the same people with whom we socialise? Do we have different discrete groups of acquaintances for our leisure activities – those with whom we have a drink and those with whom we play football? Are there times when we only mix with others of the same sex, same age and same ethnic background? Or do we combine some or all of these factors? How many of our friends and acquaintances know each other; to what extent do our personal social networks overlap? Answers to these questions give the sociolinguist a clearer idea of which factors help create the speech varieties used.

■■ Consider these different social interactions and speculate on the ways in which they may influence the way we speak. To assist you in this discussion you will find Milroy (1987) invaluable for explaining the ideas of social networking. Discuss why sometimes group pressures encourage us to maintain our distinctive speech variety, because we feel pride or confidence in being recognised or being different. However, on other occasions we hide our identity as we move towards the speech of those with whom we are interacting, perhaps to achieve acceptance in a group, or perhaps because we feel the need to 'tone down' non-standard features. Notice that in both these cases we are acknowledging our perception of the prestige of the language variety towards which we are shifting. Can you think of examples of situations where these pressures might operate? Consider, for example, the different ways in which teenagers might speak at home, to their teachers, in the playground, at a football match, when going for a job interview.

Particular types of network patterns reinforce particular speech behaviour, which may include the extent to which the group's dialect varies from the standard dialect, or the extent to which speakers alter their speech varieties, and show themselves clearly to be capable of operating in more than one dialect. Those people who operate in contexts which bring them into complex social networks will be open to far more influences and pressures that might ultimately change their form of speaking, whereas those with relatively simple networks will tend to reinforce their original dialect.

Below is a discussion of an example of where the application of network methods seems a useful way of identifying speech patterns and dialects.

Madrid: Vallecas and chabolismo

In a programme filmed by the BBC in 1979 on *chabolismo* (shanty town conditions) on the outskirts of Madrid, a series of interviews with the community involved give us some interesting examples of social and linguistic networking.

During the forties and fifties, attracted by employment prospects, poor unemployed labourers from Andalusia arrived in Madrid in large numbers. While initially at least they usually found work, there was a dreadful shortage of housing, with the result that cheap makeshift shanty settlements grew up around the industrial suburbs of Madrid. These communities were inevitably very tight-knit, concentrated groups of Andalusian origin. They brought with them their Andalusian dialects and Andalusian ways.

In the interviews we see discussion of the progress made through well-organised and well-supported political pressure on the authorities to improve the social conditions of the area, Vallecas, and in particular to build better housing. A series of short interviews takes place with two house-wives, two children, a young solderer and his wife, four local community leaders, the bishop for the area and the town hall official responsible for responding to their demands.

What emerges is that the two housewives (one about sixty and the other probably in her early forties) and the two children (eleven and thirteen) have clearly identifiable Andalusian accents. One of the children has recently arrived in the *barrio*, but the other has lived there all his life. The two women have obviously lived there for a long time.

Alberto Jacomé is a young man probably in his late twenties whose profession is solderer. With the help of his wife (who does not say any-thing during the interview!), he has designed and built his new luxurious flat, using materials from wherever he can find them, to move on from the typical *chabola*. His accent is predominantly that of Madrid and he is articulate in his answers.

All four of the men who are active in the residents' association, where the left-wing political parties are supported and prominent, are articulate and give many rousing public speeches, as well as talking to the media and the authorities. They are, nonetheless, socially and ethnically, very much part of the community, and have lived there for many years. All have predominantly Madrid-type accents, although the two older ones have slight hints of Andalusian features. In particular this could be said of Felix Rey, who actually explains to the interviewer how his community is under-educated, with low literacy rates and, as in his case, inadequate numeracy skills.

The bishop has a very standard Castilian way of speaking, in an accessible but educated style. The civil servant also uses educated standard Castilian, but what is noticeable with his answers is the highly bureau-cratic language he uses, a language which may initially have been very alien to the *chabolistas*. His name alone suggests to us that he is from a very middle class background, Luis Enríquez de Salamanca.

■■ On the basis of this brief summary of the interviews (or, better still, by watching Programme Four of *Realidades de España*), try to analyse why these people speak the way they do. What seems to be the influence of age, gender and profession? Remember the role of the political parties, which tend to be centralised national parties. There is a great sense of solidarity in this community and much communal living. Try speculating on what each of these individual's social networks might look like and where they would interlink with others'. Can you make generalisations about who is more likely to have complex social networks and why?

In the following chapter we will see what attitudes exist and how important they are as regards the different dialects and accents of Spanish.

Further reading

For further information on the dialects of Spain see Díez, Morales and Sabín (1977), and for Latin America, Lipski (1994). For a discussion of regional and social dialects in general see Wardaugh (1992), and from a historical perspective, Burke and Porter (1987). For the best discussion on language networks, see Milroy (1987). For the video of *chabolismo* in Vallecas, see BBC (1979), *Realidades de España*, Programme Four.

• • •

Language
attitudes

Chapter 5

AS WE HAVE ALREADY SEEN (for example in Chapter 2), although language experts stress the absence of any evidence that languages are in any way superior or inferior to one another, nonetheless, it is very clear that people do hold different views on the value of languages. The study of these views involves understanding and analysing language attitudes. We can divide the areas of study into three broad questions:

– what variables might affect language attitudes?
– what methods are used to measure language attitudes?
– in what areas affecting language are attitudes important?

Concentrating on this final question, we could list the following areas:

– in the evaluation of different language varieties, dialects, accents or style;
– in different language communities and groups;
– in language minorities;
– in learning languages, the learning of a particular language, and language teaching methods.

■ On a typical day consider what different language varieties you encounter. How many of the situations listed above could you test in your own experience on a routine day? Do you live and/or work where many different accents are heard, or even different languages used? Are you learning a language, and if so, why? How much of the way people around you speak do you believe influences your assumptions about these people?

Large urban areas are more likely to contain within them a wide diversity of language varieties, including different languages. A resident of Lima or Barcelona will hear different varieties of Castilian, as well as non-Castilian languages, throughout their working day. They will certainly make assumptions about the people they meet once they hear them talk. This may only be to judge from what region or country a person comes, but it might also include guessing the professional and educational background of the speaker, and even what sort of character they have.

There are particular variables which both affect the judgement of the listener and help create a picture of the person speaking.

■ Make a list of the factors that would influence your reactions to people around you on the basis of the way they speak. For example, do your own ethnicity, gender, age, educational achievement, social class or language experiences influence the way you interrelate with people?

■■ Can you think of reasons as to why language attitudes can be so important in our daily lives? For example, how, in your experience, have they affected education curricula and the training of teachers? What languages have you been taught and why? What languages have not been available to you? How do you change the way you speak when you are trying to persuade someone? In what way do politicians have to be careful about the language they use? Would you expect to speak differently if you were taking part in a job interview? Do you find some regional accents easier to understand than others, and if so, why?

In answering some of these questions you will realise how closely language attitudes are bound up with regional, social and cultural stereotypes. People from different cultural environments will have different reactions to these factors and will create different stereotypes. In this chapter we are interested in seeing what the influencing factors and stereotypes are in Spanish-speaking environments.

In an article in *El País* (13.VI.95) under the heading '*La enseñanza del habla, una lucha contra los vicios adquiridos en la familia y el barrio*', some of these attitudes and prejudices are apparent. The article describes a prize-awarding ceremony for a group of teachers who have been active in improving standards of speaking in their classrooms. The article concludes by saying:

> . . . los vicios de expresión de los padres, el entorno de los barrios y el medio social juegan un papel muy importante. 'Depende de unas zonas u otras, se habla mejor o peor, y eso hay que corregirlo, porque, si no hablan bien, tampoco escribirán correctamente cuando vayan

subiendo en el sistema escolar', afirma Odilia Baldonedo, convencida de que en los últimos años se está descuidando el léxico, 'y la televisión tiene una gran responsabilidad'.

We can see here many examples of the factors which influence language attitudes, which may or may not actually influence language itself, but are certainly perceived to do so. There is, to begin with, an assumption that there is a 'right' way to speak, deviation from which produces '*vicios*'. It is, therefore, seen as a social, and above all, an educational duty to correct 'bad' speech. The reasons for not speaking '*correctamente*' are judged to come from a variety of sources: family ('*los padres*'), geography ('*unas zonas u otras*', '*el entorno de los barrios*'), social group ('*el medio social*'), and the media ('*la televisión tiene una gran responsabilidad*'). Implicit, too, is the belief that performance in written and spoken language are linked, which may or may not be the case. The awards to the teachers underpin society's belief in the role of education as the focus for correcting language behaviour. The teacher also associates '*descuidando*' vocabulary with the influence of television. All of which emphasises a conviction of the need and value of standard norms and rejection of diversity or deviation from these. This notion of right–wrong and of norms is often in conflict with the reality of linguistic change. Language is a dynamic natural phenomenon which cannot be artificially reified, despite many efforts by those such as language academies to 'fix' it with prescribed norms. Language attitudes are often driven by a sense of the infallibility of these rules and are not always comfortable with change.

Language attitudes in the Spanish-speaking world

In the Spanish-speaking world perhaps the clearest example of this reverence for the standard form regardless of real social behaviour is found in the constant sense of inferiority expressed by so many thousands of speakers of Spanish the world over when comparing the variety they speak with that of the Castilian Spanish of central Spain. It is not just Andalusians or Catalan mother-tongue speakers talking Castilian who will insist they do not speak 'proper' Spanish, but, also, many speakers of Latin American varieties who still believe that there is a correct norm from which their variety has deviated. Clearly these attitudes have been instilled by centuries of prescriptive educational norms, by the Castilian political elites dominating cultural circles (the Madrid government both from its position as the capital of Spain, and, for many years, of the Empire), or by an eurocentric sense of superiority. There is no justification for these attitudes in purely linguistic terms – other varieties of Spanish are no less able to serve the functions of their communities – but the beliefs prevail.

An illustrative study of these attitudes towards standard Peninsular Spanish in contrast with a clearly definable Latin American variety was carried out in Argentina by Carlos Solé (in Klee and Ramon-García 1991: 92–112). Given the fact that Argentinian Spanish is very markedly different from central Peninsular Spanish, the study set out to discover what prestige and status the Argentinian variety had. On the one hand, people were asked to rate their form of Spanish in relation to other forms, and in particular to the Spanish of central Spain, and, on the other, the value they put on their language in terms of their own identity, as Argentinians. The survey was conducted in Buenos Aires (whose residents are known as '*porteños*' and speak '*porteño*'). The low esteem in which the local variety of Spanish is held is striking, with 59 per cent of the population considering it '*mal español*'. When asked if Spanish was spoken better outside Argentina, 48 per cent agreed (and of the remainder only 18 per cent said 'no', the rest having no opinion). Table 5.1 shows how the variety of Spanish spoken in Buenos Aires is compared with that of other major Spanish-speaking capital cities; it is notable that Madrid carries by far the highest value with 42 per cent.

TABLE 5.1 Value given to the speech variety of Buenos Aires as opposed to other Spanish varieties outside Argentina

Muestra total	
Madrid	42%
Bogotá	13%
Ciudad de México	10%
Lima	7%
Varios otros países[1]	15%
Sin opinión[2]	13%

1 Se agrupan aquí varios otros países de habla española mencionados por los encuestados pero con porcentajes inferiores al 5% de la encuesta total.
2 Este porcentaje incluye a esos encuestados que no mencionan ningún país específico sino que advierten que no existe tal cosa como 'mejor' español, sino 'diferente' español.

Source: Solé 1991: 112

Perhaps, however, most significant of all is the fact that despite the low rating given to the status of the Spanish of Buenos Aires by its inhabitants, they nonetheless considered their form of language as very important in the expression of their identity. Eighty-three per cent considered it a marker of their national identity, and placed it just behind 'tradition/culture' as the second most important marker of their identity, well ahead of 'religion' in third place.

■■ Bearing in mind this contrast between the low value given the status of Argentinian Spanish but the high value given it as a part of being Argentinian, discuss how language attitudes may help create a sense of group solidarity. Do we have shared national stereotypes based on language, which lead us to have certain expectations about people's place in the national community? Can you think of examples of this in your own speech community and in any Spanish-speaking ones?

It is often said that to become a British Prime Minister it is essential to speak standard English with an RP accent.

■ **Received Pronunciation** (RP) is a very British phenomenon. It refers to a particular accent which is favoured by the elites of British society and is not tied to any regional or geographical area. What are other terms used to describe this accent? Do these alternative names tell you something about the institutions and status associated with speakers of this accent?

In contrast to this belief (justified or not), Felipe González, for over fourteen years Spain's Prime Minister, has an easily recognisable Andalusian accent. It would seem that in Spain, to have an identifiable regional accent does not carry with it the same kind of stigma as say, a Yorkshire accent might carry in Britain. Such a generalisation obviously needs to be tested.

■■ If this were true, how can we explain, for example, the different accents noted in the Madrid case discussed in the previous chapter? Why do those members of the community most in contact with people and bodies outside the *barrio* show greater signs of losing their Andalusian accents than the housewives and children who are mostly limited to interaction within this local community? Discuss the importance of language attitudes to language networks.

Change in language behaviour usually implies adjustments or accommodation to a group perceived as more desirable, of higher status, and so on.

Extensive research has been done over the years to elicit accurate language attitude studies. These vary from informal, **ethnographic** interviewing, to attitude questionnaires, to more elaborate methods of testing for spontaneous, natural attitudes. The best known of the latter methods is the Matched Guise Test (originally proposed by Lambert *et al.* 1960 and thereafter considerably elaborated, see, for example, Fasold 1984).

The original Matched Guise Test consisted of an experiment whereby speakers of more than one language (e.g. Castilian and Catalan) would read or talk about the same subject in their different languages. Listeners would then be asked to rate a series of characteristics of the speakers on a scale of favourable to bad. It was found that normally the listeners would not even identify the fact that a speaker was used more than once, with the result that the same person was frequently given quite differing ratings, apparently on the basis simply of what language variety they spoke. Many variations of this test have been developed, including the use by the speakers of totally different languages, or merely different accents of the same language. Sometimes a reading text is used, while on other occasions, the speaker is asked to talk about a subject more spontaneously.

From such tests it is hoped to understand how prejudices and stereotypes about the assumed background of the speaker will lead the listener to particular conclusions. This background might be, for example, regional/national or social/educational or age or gender. Popular stereotypes such as Catalans being '*cerrados*' and '*peseteros*' or Andalusians being '*alegres* and '*llenos de gracia*' or Argentinian men '*fuertes*' and '*simpáticos*' may translate themselves into ratings for personality characteristics which apply these stereotypes. Other social stereotypes may also need testing: are Andalusians (easily identified by their accents) generally expected to be working-class, under-educated migrants who would not, therefore, have prestigious jobs? Do we presume that anyone who speaks with a Cuban accent is a dangerous revolutionary?

Some studies have been conducted to investigate attitudes to speakers of non-Castilian languages in Spain, and to understand attitudes to the minority languages spoken there. Ros *et al.* (1988) carried out a major questionnaire and matched guise test amongst respondents from five of the Spanish Autonomous Communities (Basques, Castilians, Catalans, Galicians and Valencians). Those listening to these different speakers, who were reading a weather forecast in each of their five mother tongues, were asked to attribute a series of social traits to them. Of the sixteen categories offered the most commonly chosen included:

> *Competence and achievement*: Intellectual (e.g. intelligent–stupid), cultural and professional.
> *Sociability*: Relational traits (e.g. rough–gentle; nice–unpleasant; warm–cold).
> *Personality*: Personality traits not included in the previous category.
> *Morality*: Traits that involve a clear moral evaluation (e.g. mean–generous; selfish–altruist; honest–deceitful).
> *Identity*: National identity or identification. Cultural identity. Active defence of language or culture. Language as a sign of identity.
>
> (Ros et al. 1988: 98)

The test's findings about the five linguistic groups are summarised by its authors as the following:

> . . . Galicians are viewed as politically conservative, rural, lacking in competence and very sociable. They are positively assessed in moral traits and perceived as having cultural identity. Catalans are described as competent, but unsociable. They are seen as unkind and they are thought to feel superior. They are also viewed as stingy . . . [they have] a strong group identity and a tendency to reject out-groups. Basques are described negatively in sociability traits . . . The other common dimension . . . is their identity. The image of Valencian speakers consists mainly of sociability and other positive personality traits . . . Castilian speakers have a rather neutral image . . . their outlook is that of a group conceived . . . as a melting pot.
>
> (Ros et al. 1988: 98–100)

■■ Discuss these results. Think about explanations for the answers given: how far are these based on groundless stereotypes? To what extent do you think that being a non-native Castilian speaker produces negative or positive reactions? Does there seem to be a link with a sense of identity and others' perceptions of a group's sociability? Are you able, also, to make any generalisations about the link between 'competence' and 'morality'? (See also Table 5.2.) Do these findings, and in particular the correlations between certain traits, accord with your experience in your own language environment?

TABLE 5.2 Dimensions of intergroup categorisation

Dimensions	Groups				
	Castilians	Catalans	Basques	Galicians	Valencians
Sociability	=	−	−	+*	+
Personality	=	+	+	=*	+
Identity	−	+*	+	+	=
Competence	+	+*	+	−	=
Morality	=	−*	+	+	+
	High ethnolinguistic vitality groups		Low ethnolinguistic vitality groups		

+ Positive evaluation   * Group with the highest frequency of occurrence in the dimension
= Neutral evaluation
− Negative evaluation

Source: Ros *et al.* 1988: 100

■■■ A Spanish matched guise test

Aims of the project

Groups of students (not more than five) should conduct a test with one or more native Spanish speakers who have lived for some time in Spain or Latin America. You should attempt both to produce some realistic results regarding language attitudes from the test, as well as a critical evaluation of your methods and the test. You may wish to look for the same sort of categories as in the project described above, or you may wish to ask your respondents to judge other characteristics of the readers, such as their place of origin, their gender, their age, their profession, and so on.

Stages of the project

1   You will need to find (at least four, up to six) native Spanish speakers from different parts of Spain and/or Latin America who will be prepared to record a tape for you. They must not be the same as those who will be listening to the tape!

2   Decide on what you will ask them to read or say: you could

use a weather forecast as in the example described above; you might give them a short story; you may prefer to use the recipe provided here.

Pasta con Pisto

Tiempo de realización, 40 minutos

Ingredientes:
400 g. de pasta, 2 tomates bien maduros, 1 calabacín, 1 cebolla, ajos, 1 huevo, aceite y sal.

Mientras se va calentando el agua para la pasta (siempre abundante con una cucharada de aceite y sal), vaya haciendo el pisto.

Antes de nada, trocee en cuadraditos todos los ingredientes por separado: los tomates sin piel, el calabacín pelado, la cebolla y dos dientes de ajo. Ponga una sartén grande al fuego con dos cucharadas de aceite y vaya echando estos ingredientes en el siguiente orden: la cebolla y los ajos (3 minutos), el calabacín (10 minutos), y el tomate (otros 10 minutos). Añada sal al final.

En la fuente donde va a servir la pasta, ponga la yema del huevo. Eche encima la pasta escurrida y bien caliente, y dé vueltas para que la yema se mezcle. Antes de servir, vierta por encima el pisto. Sirva inmediatamente.

3 In your groups, find a suitable subject(s); design questionnaires/interviews to elicit their reactions; clarify your objectives.
4 Carry out the test with the subject(s). Keep records of the exact procedure (for example language of discussions and explanations, extent of explanation about the test, environment in which it is carried out, details about subject(s).
5 Analyse your data from the test and any interviews.
6 Discuss the project as a whole. Evaluate the technique's value for eliciting language attitudes, criticise any weaknesses and highlight any strengths. Recommend any changes or improvements.

To carry out this sort of investigation well, we need to be very alert to possible pitfalls in the methods used.

■■   What did you discover to be some of the shortcomings of your
test? What are the potential problems of using reading as a way of
evaluating people's language? What are the particular risks of
using, for example, a recipe? Think about the quality of recordings
and the physical environment in which any test or interviews were
carried out. Do you know your subjects? What is their linguistic background and level of awareness? Do people try consciously to avoid
making stereotypical responses even when these would be their
spontaneous reactions?

One particularly common result when analysing the responses to these
types of tests is that very often subjects do not actually recognise speakers
of the same linguistic variety as their own, whilst noting other – perhaps
more well-known – forms accurately.

■■   How correct were the answers to your test? What factors might lead
subjects to make inaccurate answers? Does the order of the questions influence them in how they reply? (I.e. do certain personality
characteristics once chosen then seem to lead on to associated
stereotypical decisions about profession and place of origin, or vice
versa?)

Manuel Alvar carried out an experiment in Cuba to discover attitudes to
and knowledge about different forms of Spanish amongst Cubans. The
method was similar to the matched guise test discussed above (although
he refers to it as a '*cinta-estímulo*' (Alvar 1986: 175) with recordings of
readings by two Spaniards with 'standard' central accents, two
Andalusians, and two Cubans. Although most of his informants were of
medium- to well-educated status, their ability to identify the accents is
interesting. Whilst most of the informants were able to identify the
Peninsular Spanish without hesitation, few recognised their own compat-
riots, tending to describe them as 'Nicaraguan' or, simply, 'Latin
American'. It is possible that the close relations between Cuba and
Nicaragua during the Sandinistas' radical reforms may account for why so
many suggested this variety. On the other hand, for many years Cuba was
very isolated from other Latin American contact as the result of political
pressure. When asked which form of Spanish they preferred, over 60 per
cent opted for the form which they had (correctly) identified as Peninsular
Spanish.

In his conclusions to this study, Alvar makes some interesting observations about the important relationship between language, language attitudes and social behaviour:

> Qué duda cabe que todas estas actitudes pertenecen a una conducta social mucho más amplia que la puramente lingüística, pero no cabe duda de que la lengua es – ahora también – espejo y portavoz de otros comportamientos. Más aún, sin el lenguaje, difícil sería que manifestaran tales conductas, pues el lenguaje es instrumento de propaganda, tanto y más que la imagen, y es instrumento de identificación, como puedan serlo – y más aún – el paisaje o los deseos de libertad. Actitudes que se reflejan en el lenguaje, claro está, pero que si ese lenguaje no se manifestara de una manera muy precisa el resto de los comportamientos perderían su posibilidad de transmitirse.
>
> (Alvar 1986: 197)

Besides the importance that speakers hold towards the status of languages in terms of the standard form, the vitality of the language is another factor also affected by language attitudes. This becomes of particular importance to language planners and those planning education curricula (see Chapters 10 and 11). One way that these attitudes have a significant effect is if they are negative towards minority or minoritised languages, and thus are an obstacle in the promotion and expansion of these languages. This has frequently been the case in the Spanish-speaking world, from Galicia in Spain to the attempts to extend the use of some of the indigenous languages in Latin America.

Lastra (1992) describes some of the language attitude studies that have been undertaken in Spanish-speaking contexts. She states that not many have been carried out to date in Latin America, but mentions three where the vitality of the indigenous language as shown in language attitudes has been studied, in Peru, in Paraguay and in Chile. The Chilean study, undertaken by Fernández and Hernández in 1984, examined the attitudes of Mapuche speakers to their mother tongue and to Spanish. These speakers learn Mapuche (an indigenous language found in Chile and Argentina) at home and then Spanish at school, and all were convinced of the importance of Castilian for life in the cities. In this study, it was not age or education which influenced attitudes so much as place of residence. As Lastra reports,

> Parece que los mapuches han desarrollado una forma cíclica de acercamiento a la sociedad mayoritaria en la escuela y en las

relaciones comerciales, para luego ir retornando a lo rural y con esto a lo mapuche.

(Lastra 1992: 423)

■■ Do you think that these attitudes are likely to be generalisable to other parts of Latin America? Discuss this idea that people return to using their mother tongue after they have completed their education and established themselves. What significance might this have on inter-generational spread when and if it occurs?

Whilst experience tells us that in many situations the dominant language, such as Spanish in Latin America, is accorded prestige and status by mother-tongue speakers of indigenous languages, this is not always an unambiguous situation. Hill (1989) reports on a study she carried out in a Nahuatl-speaking community in Mexico which demonstrated that people believed that Spanish was the language to use in public domains and situations of power, such as politics or commercial transactions. And yet she documents how these people also hold clearly ambivalent attitudes towards Spanish and their language (which they call '*mexicano*') and gives examples of how Spanish is used for swearing and, in particular, as the 'nonsense' language of drunks. Nahuatl is, on the other hand, the language of such formal situations as the exchange of vows at marriage and on pledging to become *compadres*. A common situation emerges, then, whereby attitudes towards the prestige language are those of recognition of status but little real respect. In contrast the use of the mother tongue often inspires solidarity and positive feelings. Even so attitudes towards the mother tongue remain ambiguous, as these speakers are well aware of their communities' low prestige and marginalisation with which their mother tongue is inevitably associated.

■■■ On the basis of the discussions in this chapter, consider how language attitudes are likely to influence the teaching of Quechua in Bolivia; the transmission of television broadcasts in Galician in Galicia; or the language behaviour of politicians in the Spanish-speaking world.

Further reading

For a general introduction to language attitudes, see Ryan and Giles (1982) (which includes one paper on Hispanic language attitudes); Fasold (1984); and Edwards (1985). For a brief overview of language attitude studies in the Spanish-speaking world, see Lastra (1992). For examples of some interesting language attitude studies, see Alvar (1986). Woolard has carried out many fascinating studies of language attitudes in Catalonia, for example, Woolard (1989 and 1991).

•　　•　　•

Chapter 6

Register
in Spanish

While regional dialect reveals where we come from and social dialect what our status is, register gives a clue about what we are doing.

(Romaine 1994: 20)

I N CHAPTERS 4 AND 5 we looked at how dialects are indicators of both geographical and social origins, and how this knowledge can influence people's behaviour and opinions. In this chapter we are going to examine another determiner of the variety of a language spoken: **register**. As the quotation above suggests, this is entirely context-related. Register refers to the *appropriate* language for a particular context and linguistic environment. Although register and style are sometimes used in a similar way, style is an objective description of a given variety of language, irrespective of context, whereas register acknowledges the user's (usually unconscious) 'correct' variety of language for the particular context, i.e. its appropriateness.

■   Think about the different kind of language you might use to ask some-one to stop talking or making a noise. For example, you might say 'Shut up' (or something stronger); 'Be quiet'; 'Please stop talking'; 'I can't hear'; 'Could you be a little quieter please'; 'I'm sorry but would you mind not talking for a minute?', and so on. Decide which of these you might use in the following situations, and discuss why and how they differ from each other.

–   with a friend;
–   with your younger brother or sister;
–   with your teacher;
–   with the person sitting next to you in the cinema;
–   with the people around you in an airport lounge.

Imagine each of these situations both when you are feeling angry or nervous. Does this make a difference to which expression you choose?

So many different variables determine what would be appropriate language for a given situation: how well we know those with whom we are interacting, their age and gender, the formality of the situation in which we find ourselves. We will express the same idea differently if we are saying it than if we are writing it. We will use different vocabulary according to the situation; we will use non-verbal language to reinforce our point, be it body language, visual signs, graphics, and so on. Getting the appropriate expression or word to convey what you mean is extremely subtle and discriminating. It is probably the hardest aspect of language learning for non-native speakers. This is partly, too, because every language has different words and expressions for reacting differently in a given cultural context. Simply translating literally can often ignore sensitivity to register and give quite the wrong impression.

■   For example, translate the following Spanish sentence literally into English, and decide whether it would be acceptable in an English café. A normal and totally acceptable way to order a coffee in a bar in Spain would be:

> ¡Oye, chico, traeme un café!

There is no need to say '*por favor*', no need to elaborate 'politely'. Facial expressions and body language will imply friendliness. Both parties know that this is a normal interchange. If, however, you did feel the circumstances required a more 'polite' request, you might well say:

> Camarero ¿me trae un café, por favor?

Translate this sentence literally into English. Does it make sense? How would you say these two sentences in an English context?

In order to understand more clearly what influences these choices of expression and vocabulary, it is useful to divide the concept of register into three categories and then discuss what factors affect each of these. The categories are those of **field**, **tenor** and **mode**.

Field

The language employed, and particularly the precise vocabulary, will reflect the activity and subject matter of the context. If you heard someone talking about 'surfing the net and clicking on a menu' you would know that they were neither on a sunny beach in California, nor about to eat with a noisy spoon! The combination of 'surf' with 'the net' and 'click' with 'menu' would tell you that this is computer-talk and you could conjure up the situation being described. Words can, therefore, have completely different meanings according to the combinations in which they are used and the context. Not to use these words could seem clumsy, quaint or ignorant. You would certainly display computer illiteracy to talk about 'pushing the button down' instead of 'clicking' or 'the list of different things you can choose from' instead of 'menu'.

Field, then, is about the right choice of word for the situation. Often it refers to terminology or jargon. It might also, however, refer to particular grammatical style. A recipe is usually written in the form of commands, often, in Spanish, by using the infinitive form. Legal and bureaucratic documents often have very long sentences with many embedded clauses and elaborate ways of expressing ideas. In the case of some legal documents in Spanish the future subjunctive is used (which is otherwise never normally heard nowadays).

■ Consider the following sections from the law on bankruptcy and insolvency:

> El que se alzare con sus bienes en perjuicio de sus acreedores, será castigado con las penas de presidio menor, si fuere comerciante, matriculado o no; y con la de arresto mayor, si no lo fuere.
> (Hickey 1977: 103)

'Alzare' (from alzar) and 'fuere' (from ser) are both examples of the future subjunctive. Can you work out a rule for their form and use? Can you think of any special features of English 'legalese' (for example, the lack of any commas)?

■ What would the field be of a written piece which began 'muy señor mío' and ended 'le saluda atentamente'? Compare this with the English equivalent and notice how a literal translation would be ridiculous.

■ Read the following text about a forthcoming auction (*subasta*), which appeared in the Spanish *Boletín Oficial del Estado*, the Government's official organ, and then try re-writing it as if it was a note written to a friend giving them the necessary information.

> Dicha subasta tendrá lugar en la Sala Audiencia de este Juzgado de Primera Instancia número dos de los de Madrid, sito en la calle del General Castaños, número uno, señalándose para la misma, el día diecinueve de julio próximo, y hora de las doce de su mañana.
>
> (Hickey 1977: 108)

Tenor

Whilst field determines appropriate language as a result of the subject or activity being discussed, tenor responds to the relationship created between those interacting in the linguistic exchange. As we have commented already, language will alter according to the age, social status, familiarity and maybe gender of the participants. And as well as these factors, the mood and emotions of the interlocutors will influence the choice of language.

■■ If you are feeling angry, what sort of language might you use, or *not* use? Think about the use of ironic over-politeness when we are cross. Is this particularly culturally linked? Do you think all cultures use irony, understatement, sarcasm and over-politeness in the same way? Do some languages involve the use of non-verbal gestures more than others? Why should we be particularly careful about using swear words in a language which is not our mother tongue? Why do foreigners often sound so foreign when they swear in English? Discuss how important these potential pitfalls of the tenor aspect of register might be for foreign language teaching.

Any linguistic communication has, consciously or unconsciously, a sense of the degree of formality/informality, status (superiority/inferiority/equality), of politeness and respect, or of other emotions such as anger, mockery, solidarity or affection. Consciousness of this aspect of language can, in fact, be used to increase the extent of any of these effects. For example, advertisers will seek to create relationships that inspire trust, or promote desirability, encourage competition or simply flatter – all in order to persuade the public to buy their product. Politicians also need to understand how language can influence their credibility and effectiveness. Comedians may well deliberately misuse register to create comic effect. We will return to look at media examples of some of these in Chapter 7.

As we have stressed throughout, getting the right tenor or creating the appropriate relationship with the right language varies significantly from language to language. The differences between English and Spanish are no exception. It is also very important to stress that in the same way as differences occur between different national speakers of English (British, Americans, Australians, etc.) so too should we be alert to differences between the many distinct speakers of Spanish (Mexicans, Chileans, Argentinians, Spaniards, etc.). We will concentrate here on one particular area of difference which is that of how we address one another. If we return again to the example of ordering a coffee in a bar, we are reminded that even the grammatical forms used to address people will vary from language/culture to language/culture. For example, in (British) English a stark use of the **imperative** form to request something from someone we do not know particularly well would normally be considered rude and arrogant. We do not tend to say 'give me', 'do that' but instead use **modal verbs** to say such things as 'will you give me' or 'would you be so kind as to . . . '. Clearly these latter two examples should not be translated by the Spanish future or conditional verbal forms. Similarly, too much over-use of a translated 'please' or 'thank you' can produce amusement or, worse, irritation. Also, translating 'can', etc., if its function in English is as a modal verb to express politeness, by forms of *poder*, apart from sounding odd and 'foreign' might even produce the reaction of '*sí que puedo*', i.e. 'yes, I'm able to'!

■ Go back to the task at the start of this chapter on ways of asking someone to stop talking. Now think of all the different ways you might say this in Spanish, noting to whom you would say them and in what situation.

What you call someone when you address them is also important and varies from country to country, as well as from generation to generation. In Spanish it is much more normal than in English to include a name for what the person is. For example, you might well address the person as '*camarero*', whereas you are most unlikely to say 'waiter', which gives a somewhat autocratic tenor to the relationship. In many parts of Latin America titles are considered extremely important and are used whenever possible when directly addressing someone. You will therefore frequently hear '*doctor*' or '*licenciado*' or '*abogado*', and so on when someone is being directly spoken to. It is common too when talking to relatives in Spanish to call them '*hermana*', '*primo*', etc. in a way not normally used in English.

However, one of the most significant areas to analyse and understand in terms of differences between languages when creating the tenor of the relationship is the choice of personal pronouns and corresponding verb forms. How to translate the English 'you' is a very sensitive issue and one that far from relying on simplistic grammar-book rules benefits from an appreciation of the tenor aspect of register.

■■ Remind yourself of the different forms used to translate 'you' into Spanish: the singular and plural forms, the formal/informal forms, and what their corresponding verb form, (in)direct pronoun, and possessive adjective are. Remember that in most of the Spanish-speaking world, '*ustedes*' is the plural for both '*usted*' and '*tú*'. '*Vosotros/as*' is only found in standard European Spanish, and even here, much of southern Spain and the Canary Islands do not use this form.

   Vos is used in much of Latin America, instead of or as well as *tú*. Usually the object pronoun, however, is *te* and the possessive adjective *tu*. The verb form used with *vos* varies and can be a stressed form of the usual second person singular endings (e.g. *-ás*, *-és* or *-ís*) or the same as the usual second person singular endings. The plural of *vos* is *ustedes*. Why do you think so many standard Spanish grammar books or courses of Spanish for foreigners omit to explain the *vos* form?

Traditionally foreign language learners of Spanish were taught that the informal 'you' forms are used when 'one is on first-name terms' (Butt and Benjamin 1988: 126). This leads to the generalisation of such situations as: when addressing friends, family members, children, animals and God (Butt and Benjamin 1988). However, Butt and Benjamin do warn that one should be careful of over-generalisations, and Batchelor and Pountain (1992) indicate some important additions which would nowadays be normal in Spain (but not necessarily in Latin America). These are:

- among young people, whatever the circumstances;
- among people of different ages in almost any informal situation;
- addressing priests;
- wherever it is desired to establish a friendly note, even in 'semi-formal' situations (shops, banks, restaurants, etc.);
- in public speeches, especially by politicians to their audiences;
- in advertisements when a 'matey' tone is required.

(Batchelor and Pountain 1992: 283)

The deliberate flouting of these expected uses can produce subtle differences. For example, to use *usted* with someone in one of the 'semi-formal' situations mentioned above may in fact imply rebuke, irritation, superiority, or a general distancing of the speaker. Equally to use *usted* with those in an inferior position in hierarchical situations may be a deliberate sign of respect.

It must, however, be stressed that those situations described above refer particularly to Spain. One important phenomenon of post-Franco Spain has been the increased use of the informal forms. During the later Franco years *tú* and *vosotros* were increasingly used amongst those opposed to the regime as a form of solidarity and comradeship. *Usted* was associated with the values of the traditional family of hierarchical Francoist Spain. Once the dictatorship had come to an end the use of *tú* and *vosotros* was identified with the opening up of the country, with freedom in public life and with change in general. This has had a major impact on peninsular Spanish, and can be observed to differing degrees throughout the country, to some extent depending on the political colour of the region.

■■■ Try to find native Spanish speakers from different parts of the world to investigate if this is a linguistic phenomenon experienced in other parts of the Spanish-speaking world. Do you know whether speech habits changed in post-revolutionary Cuba or Nicaragua, or in Allende's Chile? This should be a task you set yourself when you are visiting or living in Spanish-speaking countries, in order to be sure that you use the 'you' system correctly.

The use of the *voseo* is often overlooked in Spanish grammar books for foreign learners. Part of the problem is the fact that its use varies considerably. The *voseo* is found in common use in Argentina, Paraguay, Uruguay, and (much of) Central America. It is rarely heard in Cuba,

Puerto Rico, (most of) Mexico, Peru or Bolivia. In Ecuador, Venezuela, Colombia and Chile its use is less common and often associated more specifically with inferior social status. Nonetheless, as with the use of *tú* in Spain, it is dangerous to over-generalise, and better to acknowledge the constantly changing nature of language which reacts so significantly to social, cultural and political circumstances. One further variation on the appropriate 'you' form in Latin America is found with the use in some areas of *usted* for the most intimate relationships of all. This is the case, for example, in Venezuela and Costa Rica, where parents call their children *usted*.

To use the Spanish address system accurately, then, it is essential to be aware of how relationships are linguistically created. An understanding of register allows us to move on from the prescriptiveness of grammatical rules and to notice exceptions and changes, and to choose the most appropriate option.

Mode

The third category of register, besides deciding what subject or activity is taking place, or with whom one is interacting, is that which defines the means of communication being used, that is the mode. These channels of communication may be verbal through speech, or graphically transmitted, which in many Western societies implies through writing systems. However, writing systems vary widely, and not all languages share the alphabets used by English and Spanish. Writing is not used universally as the only way to portray language visually.

- What systems other than writing have been used to communicate ideas in some graphical or symbolic form? Of significance to us, both the Aztec and Inca Empires had developed such systems to communicate messages across their wide territories.

While speaking–writing is the basic dichotomy for mode in English and Spanish, there are variants and additional aspects to these two. For example, we have already noted that body language usually complements verbal communication (such as hand gestures, facial expressions and head movements) as well as non-verbal sounds.

■■   Compare (for example by watching Spanish TV) the use of hands by English and Spanish speakers. In what ways do they differ? Does it matter if you do not use hand gestures in the same way as native speakers? Are the signs and sounds used to express 'yes' and 'no' in both languages the same?

The written word is often supplemented by pictures or tables, graphs, diagrams, and so on. Moreover, in the case of written language the format and presentation will be specific to the context, and therefore appropriate for that use. For example, if you look at most newspaper items you could identify them as such immediately. Newspapers are usually published in columns, with extremely short paragraphs (quite often just one sentence) with large full line headlines at the beginning, bylines, and often short headings breaking up the columns.

■■   Take an article from any regular daily newspaper, English or Spanish, and copy it out on a piece of A4 paper with the normal font and line length of, say, an academic essay. Compare the two pieces. You will probably find that these are full of very short paragraphs, sentences which begin with words such as 'And', and a surprising absence of subordinate clauses.

Similarly you do not need to read the words on a page containing a letter to know what the function of the language is. Even allowing for different conventions between languages (where on the page the sender's address is placed, or the position of the date, etc.) you will know from the inclusion of separated addresses, introductory salutations and carefully placed endings that this is a letter.

Whereas spoken language operates from the premise that the listener is physically close and able to respond, either verbally or silently, individually or as part of an audience, and can therefore to some extent be identified, written language is more distant, and in many cases the identity of the eventual reader cannot be known. However, these are again the generalised situations, there are many modes which come somewhere in the middle. For example, a recording of a speech may well contain someone reading written language out loud. This is probably as distant from their audience as many forms of writing. A telephone conversation whilst directly in contact lacks non-verbal reactions. A new and potentially fascinating mode of communication is that of electronic mail. Already it would seem that the language used in this form of contact is neither that of letters nor that of telephone conversations. Certain register-specific conventions are becoming standard for e-mailers.

■■ If you have access to electronic mail or to the Internet, explore any Spanish-language information that you can find. Consider the style and register being used, and decide whether this seems broadly similar to (and perhaps translated from) English or whether it has features of its own.

Most commonly the spoken mode involves two or more participants, who interact in conversation or more formal dialogue (interviews etc.). The participants also follow unconscious but accepted rules of linguistic behaviour: 'turn taking', involving understood ways of interrupting, negotiating, responding, dominating and so on. This behaviour is also importantly language- and culture-specific.

■■ Consider what movements, expressions, as well as actual words are used to take part in a Spanish conversation. To do this you may find it helpful to watch Spanish-language TV. Watch how speakers join in on chat shows or when they are being interviewed for news reports and documentaries. Compare this with similar English-language situations.

As we have seen in earlier chapters, written language has often formed the basis of what is considered the standard language and comes to be seen as the correct form of a language, whilst any other variety is rejected or receives unfavourable attitudes. This leads to a prescriptive and often very restricted corpus of grammatical rules being applied to every and any situation.

■ Can you think of examples in English of when what you have said is corrected as being 'bad' English? (Such as 'split infinitives', finishing a sentence with a preposition, or saying 'It was me'.) Do these 'mistakes' really matter? Are you aware of any similar criticisms of Spanish speakers?

Written language sometimes experiences criticism from language purists, but it is in the mode of the spoken language that their battle really rages. In many ways this in fact is a misunderstanding of the fundamental difference between the two modes.

■■ One way to demonstrate this difference is to transcribe literally into written form something which has been said. To do this it is important (a) to have spontaneous spoken language, and not a pre-written script; and (b) to aim for a relatively formal situation in order to avoid extreme colloquial speech displaying linguistic features which would never be written down. Below is an example taken from the BBC documentary about the *chabolas* in Madrid (see Chapter 4).

Victor is asked by the interviewer, Pilar, to describe how the electricity cooperative works. His reply is as informative and intelligible as one would expect in a spoken interview situation. However, if the transcription of it is analysed, it displays many features which might be described as 'incorrect' grammatically.

PILAR: ¿Y la cooperativa pasa a cobrar el . . . la luz, casa por casa, al mes?

VICTOR: Sí, o sea cada . . . Luego ya cada vecino . . . O sea, el sistema ya luego es . . . normal, como si fuera en realidad . . . como si fuera una compañía . . . distribuidora, en el sentido que cada vecino tiene su propio contador individual . . . Ahí se marca lo que ha gastao ese vecino en el mes, y se le cobra eso. Las diferencias están en que . . . bueno, el precio pues viene resultando pues un diez por ciento, en el conjunto global del barrio, un diez por ciento más barato de los precios oficiales que existen . . . en las compañías eléctricas, y que, bueno, pues otras facilidades, pues que, bueno, a la hora de haber una avería, por ejemplo, pues al estar esto aquí en el mismo barrio, tener un servicio de guardia, pues . . . se suelen arreglar mucho más rápido . . . El mismo sistema de cobro, que es mensual y pasando por las casas, en vez de como obligan las compañías, que hay que ir a pagar a las oficinas o bancos o cosas raras, ¿no? . . . O sea, tienes una serie de ventajas de ese tipo, ¿no? Pero el sistema es igual que si fuera una compañía distribuidora.

(BBC 1977)

■■ Read this passage and see how many examples you can find of what is unacceptable in standard written language, but perfectly normal in standard speech. List as many categories of this difference as you can. When you have finished read the explanation given below.

This is an excellent example of a range of perfectly normal differences between spoken and written modes. To begin with, self-correction takes place as a speaker goes along, and cannot be deleted as with written language. So Pilar says 'el . . . la luz' as she adjusts to the correct gender. This kind of inaccuracy of gender or quantity (e.g. singular adjectives, plural nouns) is inevitable in a language with a high degree of **concordance**. English presents different problems, mostly connected with word order which is far tighter than in Spanish. However, even word order is affected here as can be seen in the re-phrasing that Victor goes through at the start of his response.

False starts and re-phrasing are normal in spoken language, as is also the need to use 'filler' words, words with no real meaning but which fill in pauses as thoughts are ordered. This example is full of words such as '*bueno*', '*pues*' and '*o sea*', as well as actual pauses transcribed here by three dots. Common too in speech is the need to repeat words and ideas. This may be unconscious, or deliberate, as with the natural redundancy and rephrasing that is normal in such spoken examples as lectures or speeches. When we read, if we do not immediately follow or understand something, we can re-read. You cannot, however, go over a spoken text, but all these devices – pauses, fillers, repetitions, re-wording, etc. – help the listener follow the gist.

Another aspect of spoken language is the proximity, in time and space, of the listener. For example, Victor can say '*al estar esto aquí*' in the knowledge that his interviewer, Pilar, and listeners viewing the programme, can see where '*aquí*' is and can have a shared concept of '*esto*'. Time and place can be fixed and identifiable in speech, whereas in written language there are not the same points of reference. In a similar way spoken language reacts to and elicits responses from the listener, so that Victor uses the question tags '*¿no?*' to involve Pilar, without really expecting an answer. He also uses the informal second person form '*tienes*' reflecting the relationship of the interview whereas a written explanation would be more likely to use an impersonal or more formal form.

Finally, there are many examples in this transcription of the 'ungrammaticality' of spoken language: incomplete sentences lacking finite verbs, mixed forms (e.g. ' . . . *que es mensual y pasando por las casas* . . . '), transitive verbs missing their object ('*como obligan las compañías* . . . '), or lack of agreements or confusion as to what refers to what ('*pues otras facilidades, pues que, bueno a la hora de haber una avería, por ejemplo, pues al estar esto aquí en el mismo barrio, tener un servicio de guardia, pues . . . se suelen arreglar mucho más rápido* . . . '. What or who is the subject of '*se suelen*'?).

■■ Now try re-writing Victor's answer as if it was a short paragraph in a pamphlet describing the electricity cooperative.

Apart from the need to understand these differences when learning to use a foreign language correctly and appropriately, those who seek to imitate 'real' language need to appreciate these differences. For example a film script writer or a dramatist should aim to notice and reproduce these differences if they wish their scripts to sound authentic.

■■■ Look at examples from a range of Spanish-language playwrights, over different periods in time (e.g. Valle Inclán, Lorca, Buero Vallejo), and decide how aware of different modes they really are when writing their dialogues. Listen to popular TV programmes in English and Spanish and see whether this is the case. Notice that even when the words and phrases are 'right' if the movements, facial expressions and voice intonation are not spontaneous to match, the effect will be one of artificiality. Do you think in fact that we expect some artificiality in drama-speak?

The extent to which the media consciously or unconsciously follows the conventions of register will be discussed in the next chapter.

Further reading

For a general introduction to register see Romaine (1994) or Montgomery (1986). For register in Spanish, see Batchelor and Pountain (1992) and Hickey (1977). Butt and Benjamin (1988) is a good wide-ranging grammar book of Spanish which is sensitive to issues of register.

• • •

Chapter 7
_____

Getting the
message across
Spanish
in the media

Chapter 7

As WE HAVE ALREADY NOTED in Chapter 6, understanding what language to use is very important when analysing public language, and particularly that of the media. We want not only to recognise the register of this language, particularly as foreign language learners, but also to see how far those using it are conscious of the varieties they choose and why, and to consider how influential these varieties are on language behaviour generally.

In the introduction to a selection of papers presented at a congress of the Academias de la Lengua Española in 1985 in Madrid to discuss the role of the media as regards the Spanish language, the Venezuelan Pedro Díaz Seijas wrote

> Los diferentes trabajos ... coinciden en señalar un alarmante deterioro del español al sufrir alteraciones en el uso diario que cada vez con mayor radio de acción realizan los medios de comunicación.
>
> Este es desde luego el aspecto tradicional que las Academias desde su nacimiento, han venido observando y tratando de corregir en beneficio de la conservación y la unidad del idioma en el ámbito hispanohablante.
>
> (Academia Venezolana 1986: 7)

> ■ Once again we can see the tension that we have already noted between natural language change and forces determined to protect and preserve what they view as 'correct' language from 'impurities'. Can you think of outcries of a similar sort by equally respectable groups of people in the defence of English or French, for example?

However, Díaz Seijas does go on to say that unusually for the Academies and their members, at this congress there was a visible shift in the perception of their role with some acknowledgement of the inevitability of the phenomenon of language change:

> No obstante, por primera vez ... la preocupación principal del Congreso ... fue ... el estudio concienzudo, científico a la luz de los

avances modernos de la lingüística y de la filología, acerca del complejo fenómeno producido en nuestros días por los medios de comunicación, como la radio y la televisión, cuya influencia en el campo de los usuarios tiende a cambiar con éxito las viejas estrategias establecidas para la preservación del idioma, como punto de partida de toda comunicación.

(Academia Venezolana 1986: 7–8)

In this chapter we will look at this change in the Spanish language brought about by the media, examining what are the major influences causing it, and comparing it with other major media languages. We will see how these changes inevitably reflect changes in Spanish and Latin American society in general, and in particular play an important part in the political environment of each nation. We will examine the position of television, radio and the written press, and highlight specifically some of the linguistic issues relating to advertising. The quotations from the Madrid Congress raise such questions as: is there really a '*deterioro*' in Spanish as the result of its use in the media? What is the significance of the '*mayor radio de acción*' occupied by the media? Is it desirable (or possible) to maintain the '*unidad del idioma en el ámbito hispanohablante*'?

Television

Most would agree that this is the most influential and all-pervasive amongst the different forms of the media, and is now received in the majority of the world's population centres. Whilst there are obviously still remote parts of Latin America where television cannot be received, these are few. In particular television has an important impact in urban areas as a form of communication equally accessible to poor and rich. Because television is the most popular form of media communication, those who wish to influence opinions and behaviour need to know how to use it. The media has the potential to be used to promote particular cultural and social models, as well as transmit political messages. It can, therefore, also be a conscious vehicle for language change (see Chapter 10) used by those wishing to expand the use of a particular language or variety of language.

- Can you think of any words or phrases, or pronunciation which have been regularly heard on your local television or radio which have gradually become accepted forms of speech?

Two important points need to be remembered about television: first, that it has a potentially very wide audience, often beyond specific political borders; and, second, that producing quantity and quality programmes is very expensive.

■■ Consider what the implications of these two points might be for Spanish and Latin American television? After you have had a preliminary discussion of this, read the discussion below.

In fact, as we shall see, these two factors are very closely connected. The cost of producing television programmes leads many national and private networks to buy from multinational companies rather than make their own. This tends, above all, to mean buying from US-owned companies, and, to a much lesser extent, British, French, and so on. In the Spanish-speaking world there are few television programme producers, and often these are US-finance backed. To a significant extent, both Spanish and Latin American television have to buy many American and British programmes. There are of course, very important linguistic consequences to this: much of what is seen on TV in Spanish-speaking countries is either dubbed or uses subtitles.

The linguistic problems associated with subtitles and dubbing are well known. It is difficult to re-create the authentic feel to a dubbed programme: for example, mouths and facial expressions do not synchronise, and translations tend to be clumsy in order to fit into the exact time and space on the screen. Moreover, if we consider some of the aspects of register discussed in Chapter 6 it becomes apparent that potentially cultural appropriateness varies considerably from one language to another. Dubbing frequently does not take these factors into account, with the result that, for example, body language is inappropriate for the target audience, or, remembering the issues of language attitudes in Chapter 5, the accent and language variety are not suitable for the type of character being portrayed. The Catalans have been particularly keen to promote the use of Catalan by dubbing wide-selling programmes into Catalan (see Chapter 10) with the result that such British programmes as *Yes, Prime Minister* and *EastEnders* have been dubbed. In the former the very particular body language of an upper-class British civil servant simply does not convey the same meaning when the voice speaks Catalan; in the latter, little attempt to replicate the working-class East London accent by a Catalan social equivalent has been attempted. The result is similar to hearing Shakespearean actors' accents and voices interpreting East End working-class characters!

Despite its difficulties and frequent criticisms of its deficiencies, dubbing is the far more common form of presenting non-Spanish programmes in the Spanish-speaking world. Subtitling, which is more common in the English-speaking world, however, also presents problems.

■■ In order to understand the challenges of this practice, try producing some subtitles for yourself. A good idea is to take a short piece of Spanish which has already been subtitled, but look at it without its subtitles first. To do this you can simply stick a piece of paper over the place on the monitor where the writing will always be. An alternative is to use the wide range of excellent BBC programmes which teach Spanish (such as *España Viva*) and which frequently have the same clips with and without subtitles. When you have tried subtitling a few dialogues, compare your efforts with the professional version. Discuss the problems you have encountered.

Jorge Díaz Cintas (1995) in his article '*El subtitulado como técnica docente*' lists some of the different aspects which are essential and difficult to achieve when writing subtitles. These include: the need for 'compression' requiring good summarising skills; care to keep coherence between utterances and across the entire text/programme; suitability of the register; how to represent instantaneously more than one person talking at a time; the problem of translating non-verbal (written) background language such as on signposts, book covers, letters, and so on (Díaz Cintas 1995: 11–12).

One of the greatest challenges for dubbing and subtitling is an ever-present problem in translation: cultural specificity. We have already come across this problem when looking at the subtleties of register. Many of the examples discussed in Chapter 6 can serve again to underline the difficulties of the instant and rapid transfer, for example, of an Australian soap series to a Spanish-speaking audience, in, say, Venezuela. Which form of 'you' to use; how to translate exclamations and particularly swearing; whether to try to convey the humour intended, through irony or sarcasm, or how to deal with cultural references.

As the majority of TV programmes are produced by the large international companies, which predominantly operate in English, it becomes most important to them that the content and language should not be too culture-specific. In this sense the cost of production and the extent of audiences are linked. Even in the Spanish-speaking world producers hope that the common denominator of the Spanish language will enable companies to sell their programmes to different national networks. Again, this may lead them to avoid overly culturally specific content. From a linguistic point of view this produces a variety of issues. On the one hand, if the language used is considered at all by the producers, it may well lead to a deliberate attempt to keep to standard 'neutral' Spanish, normally favouring the variety of Spain.

■ This might enhance the *'unidad del idioma en el ámbito hispano-hablante'* that Díaz Seijas refers to, but do you think it represents authentic language in its real context?

It is, however, more common that such considerations are not even taken into account, with the result that the Spanish used is recognisably that of a particular part of the Spanish-speaking world. This can have two effects: either it may alienate the audience who do not identify sufficiently with the speakers; or this variety will start to infiltrate and influence the Spanish spoken by the target audience. The tremendous popularity in recent years of Venezuelan-produced romantic soaps has led to the impact of the Venezuelan variety of Spanish on other Spanish-speaking communities. Frequently US companies use Puerto Rican actors and translators to dub their programmes, with the result that, particularly in Spain, for many years Puerto Rican Spanish was in danger of being considered *the* Latin American Spanish, as if there were one homogeneous variety.

What we see – and this is not unique to the Spanish-speaking world – is a globalising and de-contextualising of Spanish. The more local or national peculiarities are removed or uprooted.

■■ Discuss whether you think this tendency towards a less culturally specific language in TV programmes matters? What are some of its implications?

■■ Many commentators argue that the dominance of the wealthier and more widespread languages and cultures will squeeze out the smaller ones. In the Spanish-speaking world this is often seen in terms of dominance by the USA. However, when asked if this is what is happening with Mexican culture and, in particular, in Mexican TV, the well-known Mexican writer Carlos Fuentes retorted:

. . . para nada. Yo creo que nuestra cultura es más fuerte que la de los Estados Unidos. Para empezar, a mí no me molesta ninguna relación cultural. Yo creo que las culturas viven de su

comunicación, incluso de su contagio y no de su aislamiento, eh
... México y la América Latina están teniendo una influencia
cada vez mayor en los Estados Unidos.

(BBC 1990)

Do you agree with Fuentes?

Radio

Some of what can be said about the influence of television on social, and
specifically, linguistic behaviour, can be said also about radio, but in a
more limited sense. It too has to contend with how to translate programmes designed to appeal to international audiences, although radio, on
the whole, tends to operate for a smaller and therefore more identifiable
audience. Nonetheless transmission can and does extend beyond political
borders, presenting some interesting decisions and dilemmas. As Lipski
has documented (in Klee and Ramos-García 1991: 113–137) clandestine
broadcasting has often taken place in Latin America for political reasons
with the overt purpose of transmitting an alternative political message to
that of a particular national government. He cites interesting examples of
Cuba, Nicaragua and El Salvador where the way accent, vocabulary and
register in general of these broadcasts are received by the target audience
may or may not have been given deliberate thought.

■■ Imagine a similar situation of a clandestine radio broadcast just inside
France transmitting to Spain during the Franco years. What linguistic
problems might have needed to have been addressed? Remember the
discussion about the change in the use of *tú* and *usted* during this
period. How might that affect the language of broadcasting?

Lipski describes in detail his different examples, showing where broadcasters seem to be consciously aware of the language attitudes of the target
audiences and thus make consequent adjustments. He also highlights the
link between ideological positions and ways of speaking.

■■ Read Lipski's conclusions to the research he carried out on clandestine
broadcasting, and discuss how far you feel these are applicable to
analyses of broadcast media in general.

... the behavior reflected in the present research does not suggest conscious, consistently planned modification of a single linguistic parameter by the directors and announcers of the official, nonofficial and clandestine broadcast being discussed. Rather, the linguistic profile adopted by the individuals involved stems directly and naturally from the ideological concerns of the groups they represent. That the speech of radio personnel differs significantly from local colloquial patterns comes as no surprise, nor does the concept of a station being sensitive to the impact of certain linguistic configurations on listeners. In the war of words and ideas between official outlets and rebel stations in Latin America, the situation becomes more complex, due to the simultaneous consideration of domestic and international audiences of differing ideological, sociocultural and dialectological profiles. The linguistic behavior of announcers and occasional radio personalities reflects the interaction of conscious and unconscious, voluntary and involuntary faces of language variation, as well as the multitude of external forces and influences, which affect the organisation and practices of the stations.

(Lipski 1991: 132–133)

Another way in which the language of the radio has proved important in Latin America has been in the promotion of non-Castilian indigenous languages, in particular amongst people who are illiterate in Spanish. In Guatemala and Bolivia (see also Chapters 10 and 11) this has proved an important way of improving the status of these communities and their languages. Radio broadcasting as a modern technological phenomenon gives status and prestige to marginalised groups. As Archer and Costello report (1990) the Mam-speaking community in Guatemala achieved much in the way of improving perceptions and pride in the local Mam culture and way of life when this community built and operated its own radio station. Initially the intention had been to use their transmissions to promote literacy in Mam (as they had already been doing in a limited way on state radio), but it soon became apparent to the broadcasters that the local community needed first to be won over with programmes of a more immediate purpose, such as those talking about agricultural problems and their solutions. As Archer and Costello write:

Possibly more important than even the content of the programmes was the fact that the transmissions were in a mixture of Mam and

Spanish. A language which people had been ashamed to speak in public places was suddenly being used by the only mass medium in the area.

(Archer and Costello 1990: 145)

In Bolivia too, radio broadcasting has been used as a way to promote the use of and respect for native languages other than Spanish, notably Quechua and Aymara. In the 1970s as various non-governmental organisations tried to improve literacy amongst marginalised groups and bilingual/bicultural programmes for adults and children, the use of radio was a central focus. In a similar way to the Guatemalan case, literacy was identified as being firstly the communicating of relevant topics of interest to be discussed by the indigenous populations. Until the material was relevant there would be no interest in participating in a wider educational context. Not only the content, but also the language of transmission and the methods had as their aim to involve the indigenous population.

La red radiofónica de ERBOL...[ha] ido adoptando estilos más propios del lenguaje radiofónico. Por ejemplo, se ha enfatizado el micrófono abierto a todos, y últimamente se ha creado una red de reporteros populares que periódicamente entran en cadena en todas las radios de ERBOL para informar y discutir lo que acontece en diversas partes del campo e incluso en sectores populares urbanos o mineros.

(Plaza and Albó 1989: 77)

Similarly women have learnt to use local (often clandestine) radio broadcasts to communicate their shared concerns and interests in places such as Pinochet's Chile, as we shall see in Chapter 8.

Newspapers and the written media

Written journalism has a powerful influence on language behaviour too. In particular many of the sacred rules of prescriptive grammar are ruthlessly broken by writers in the more popular press.

- Can you think of examples of this in the English-language press? Compare the language of the tabloids with the so-called quality press.

Once again we find signs of the globalising or internationalising effect of the media. Newspapers are often fed stories from international news agencies and their reports take on a recognisable format which goes beyond particular national or language boundaries. The Reuter's-style presentation of a typical front page report, with wide large headlines, followed by a summary of the article in smaller letters, but still larger than the main body of the report, followed by the main report in columns with short sentences and short paragraphs is a format which is now standard in many parts of the world.

As far as Spanish is concerned, English has had a noticeable impact on the language of journalism. One particularly obvious 'anglicisation' of Spanish found in most Spanish-language newspapers is the predominance of the passive voice, which is far less used in more traditional written Spanish. Look at the following example:

> ATENAS 29 (Efe-Reuter) – El general Panaourgias, partidario del rey Constantino, fue detenido anoche por las fuerzas de seguridad, según se dice en los medios bien informados de Atenas.
>
> El general, que tiene 54 años de edad, fue retirado del servicio activo desde 1967.
>
> En 1970 fue enviado al exilio a un pueblo remoto, por considerársele peligroso para el Gobierno, el orden público y la seguridad nacional . . .
>
> Ayer fue facilitada una nota por el Ministerio de Defensa en la que se decía que 35 jefes y oficiales . . . fueron detenidos en relación con el fracasado intento de sublevación.
>
> (*Heraldo de Aragón* 30.V.73, cited in Hickey 1977: 24)

■■ Note all the passives used here (*fue/fueron* plus past participles); change these sentences into other forms, which you might more commonly expect to find.

The word order of this extract also suggests an English original, or an Anglicised style. In particular, English tends to place adverbs or adverbial phrases of time after the verb whilst Spanish would more usually put them at the beginning. The second paragraph in particular reads uncomfortably, as the relative clause, giving the general's age, splits the subject off from the verb.

Debates about 'correct' language occur regularly when discussing the press, and take place the world over. This is certainly the case with

Spanish, both at the level of vocabulary and grammatical standards, and of style. In a recent article in the Barcelona daily *La Vanguardia* relatively strong swear words (which might also be considered blasphemous) were included in an article which reported faithfully a conversation between the journalist and a *guardia civil*. This produced many outraged letters, as well as a subsequent article in the paper defending the journalist (somewhat lukewarmly) but also printing the counter views of various eminent people. Particularly relevant is the reaction from Fernando Lázaro Carreter, president of the Real Academia Española:

> El periodista no es un fotógrafo, sino un mediador y el hecho de traducir literalmente la verdad aquí es una falta de respeto. La palabra que ha motivado las quejas de los lectores tiene un contenido inicialmente blasfemo, y, por tanto, rechazable. La reproducción de estos términos es una concesión a lo más inmediato, trivial, espontáneo y grosero, y es alarmante que se introduzca en las páginas de los diarios.

■■ Do you agree with this assertion that the journalist is not a *'fotógrafo'* of society's language but instead should mediate and interpret? By examining a range of Spanish-language newspapers and magazines, allocate articles you read into these two categories: 'linguistic photographer' or 'linguistic mediator'. In the latter category suggest what kinds of changes the journalist seems to make to the original language of the incident or interview.

The notion that the journalist consciously manipulates language for a particular purpose is certainly often the case when we analyse the role of journalism in politics. Such journalism may be as the organ of the government, or of particular political parties in a democratic society. The language chosen will then reflect the ideology associated with these. It is not difficult to recognise the ideological colour of the Cuban government on reading a publication such as *Gramna*, the national newspaper of the Castro regime. Equally strident and recognisable were right-wing media supporters of the Franco regime, such as followers of Fuerza Nueva. However, less accessible to analysis and of particular interest to the linguist are the strategies that journalists will follow in order to survive in situations of potential and powerful censorship. Spain has a long tradition of learning to live with censorship. A notable nineteenth-century writer Mariano José de Larra was famous for the degree of satire and implicit reference he developed as a journalist in his time. Perhaps it is not an exaggeration to say that the tradition goes back to one of the most famous of Spanish Golden Age writers, Francisco de Quevedo. Certainly during the Franco years those publications which attempted to question the regime in their pages had to use the utmost care and inevitably extreme obliqueness. This need to imply or make very complex indirect reference to ideas known to be shared and understood by the readership has certainly led to a very recognisable style in contemporary Spanish journalism, a style which is only just beginning to disappear more than twenty years after Franco's death. Such a degree of obliqueness and inference makes Spanish journalism highly culture-specific and often very difficult for non-Spaniards and particularly non-Spanish speakers to understand.

■■■ Try to find out (by talking to native Spanish speakers or during visits to Spanish-speaking countries) if this kind of style has been developed in other parts of the Spanish-speaking world where censorship is in operation. In particular consider the contrasting situations of Pinochet's Chile and Castro's Cuba.

The style of writing is of course only one of the ingredients that make up a newspaper or magazine. As we saw when discussing the mode aspect of register, such things as layout and illustrations are also important. Cost will be a significant factor in the quality of some of these elements, determining, for example, paper quality, photography and length.

■■ Choose any Spanish-language daily paper and analyse it from the point of view of the following quotation by Juan Luis Cebrián, former editor of Spain's widest-circulation daily *El País*:

> Textos, fotografías, dibujos, publicidad y titulares son finalmente la materia prima con la que se confecciona un periódico. Este no es una simple mezcla de todas esas cosas, sino que todas ellas deben ponerse al servicio del mensaje informativo que se quiere hacer llegar al lector. La forma de los periódicos, la estructura de sus secciones, el estilo de su narración, el tamaño de sus fotografías y titulares, el color de la tinta, la propia expresión publicitaria, son mucho antes que la selección o tratamiento de las noticias, las percepciones básicas que el lector recibe.
>
> (Cebrián 1980: 26–27)

Advertising

One of the major roles of the media is to transmit publicity and propaganda, not just of the political kind which we have already discussed, but, of course, to advertise commercial (as well as on occasion, government) products. The linguistic variety and register employed to create effective advertisements vary from language to language and from country to country. They are susceptible to many of the same influences we have noted in general as regards the mass media. For example, many of the products most fiercely marketed are those of multinational companies; their advertising campaigns may deliberately aim at a sense of 'internationalism'. It is cheaper to make one television advertisement and then dub it into diverse languages. The original language is more than likely to be English.

■■ In order to persuade potential buyers it would seem obvious that those marketing a product should think carefully about the relationship that they wish to create between the message and the potential customer. In other words, the tenor aspect of register is extremely important. Given this, can you see problems with the dubbing of English-language original advertisements into, for example, Spanish? Find some specific examples to illustrate the discussion.

Advertising represents big business, and at its most competitive is very sophisticated. Much of this sophistication comes from a subtle and clever understanding and use of the appropriate aspects of register in order to control the environment and relationship that is to be created. These aspects include the need to decide how far the advertising must be culture-specific. It may well be that multinational drinks companies or manufacturers of computers and cars feel that their products know no political (or linguistic) boundaries, but, nonetheless, even to create this feeling of belonging to a fast, sophisticated, modern world may require different stimuli in different contexts.

■ For example, such a feeling is often aimed at in English-language advertisements in Britain by the use of American accents. What similar device could Spanish-speaking advertisers use?

Recent trends in Spanish advertising show a greatly increased use of the *tú* form. This is a further reflection of the changes in linguistic usage in Spanish society as a whole, which, not surprisingly, advertisers have been quick to note. For the same reasons, these advertisements would be less successful in many parts of Latin America, as, in general, would the many Spanish advertisements which have since the death of Franco taken great pleasure in exploiting to the limits vastly more liberal and tolerant social attitudes. Sparsely dressed bodies, sexually explicit images and words have become the norm in contemporary Spain, but would be highly unsuitable in much of Latin America.

Many advertisements do contain, consciously or unconsciously, an appreciation of the cultural expectations of their audience. Spanish-language TV advertisements make far greater use of children, often with very high-pitched voices, which might even seem cloying to a British audience.

■■ Compare this, for example, to recent TV advertisements in Britain for a well-known supermarket chain, where a young boy of about two or three, seen accompanying his mother on shopping trips or helping her unpack, has his thoughts conveyed to us via an adult man's voice, producing a highly effective humorous impact which is achieved by 'breaking' the rules of register, and using an unexpected and 'inappropriate' mode of speech. Do you think a similar advertisement would be as successful in a Spanish-speaking context?

A study of British advertisements will show how often animals are employed either instead of humans (and therefore in a speaking capacity) or as part of the overall image. With the possible exception of dogs, this is far less common with Spanish-language advertisements, and seems again to point to a different attitude to animals in these societies.

Accent variation plays a very important part in the construction of British TV advertising, but is almost entirely absent from Spanish-language advertising. This indicates the difference in attitudes to social as well as regional accents in operation in these communities. A well-known Yorkshire beer is sold to us by two talking horses, speaking with Yorkshire accents in the environment of a folksy pub; chocolate buttons are sung about by cartoon animal characters using the words and music of a well-known nursery rhyme. Whereas a Spanish TV advertisement for a cheese (greatly favoured by children) shows a perfect family sitting around the kitchen table with the child asking his father the meaning of the word 'tierno', and being told that this is (a) what his mother is; and (b) what the cheese is. An advertisement for a widely sold Spanish orange juice has images of the juice and people drinking over the voice of Nat King Cole singing in English (despite the very Spanish origin associated with oranges)! The cultural contrast between these Spanish and English advertisements is enormous.

Current 'political correctness' can be monitored in advertising, showing how far advertisers feel they need to assume their buyers will take this seriously. Much will depend too on the extent to which a product is being packaged for a particular target audience, as advertisers are happy to risk alienating other sectors whom they consider to be unlikely buyers. In Chapter 8 we will look specifically at the role of women as portrayed or targeted in advertising. Here, it is worth commenting that a noticeable trend in present Spanish advertising is a consciousness of environmental 'green' issues.

■■ Take a series of English-language and Spanish-language advertise-ments, if possible both in printed and recorded forms, and compare them for the following elements:

- the voices, accents, dialects, etc.;
- background music (is it identifiable? is it only likely to be recog-nised by a particular national/cultural group?);
- quality of photography; use of computer-generated images; use of cartoon characters and graphics;
- use of humour (how is this achieved?);
- targeting of audiences (women/men? children? businessmen? families? those with money to spend?);
- creation of particular feelings and emotions: of competition, of envy, of prudence, of risks and dreams?;
- coherence of different elements (e.g. does the visual image create some kind of metaphor along with the spoken voice-over?);
- cost of the production.

Then discuss what conclusions you can draw from the differences and similarities of the two in terms of the issues raised in this chapter.

■■■ Create your own advertisement in Spanish (either written or recorded) for the following products: *Champú la Belleza, la Caja de Ahorros Popular* and *Cerveza Quítased.* Explain what you are trying to achieve and how, and whom you are targeting.

Further reading

For a brief introduction to some of the issues discussed in this chapter, see Montgomery (1986). Fowler (1991) presents a stimulating and challenging linguist's analysis of the power of language in the news. For a provocative overview from the Spanish language academies' point of view see Academia Venozolana (1988).

•   •   •

Chapter 8

Language
and gender

Chapter 8

I N T H I S C H A P T E R we will bring together some of the strands of
the other chapters of Part two, such as social influences, attitudes to
language, register and the role of the media, to see how these impact in
one particularly topical area, that of language and gender.

■ Are you aware of ways in which English marks gender? Compare
this with Spanish. Do these, or any other factors, in your opinion
make English a 'sexist' language?

This chapter will see how far Spanish, or at least the use of Spanish, can
be considered sexist. By this we mean the unequal treatment of the two
sexes through language use, normally to the detriment of women.

■■ Consider and discuss, in the context of any languages you know,
the following statement. Can you find examples of the linguistic
incidences mentioned here?

> El lenguaje es un buen ejemplo del SEXISMO cultural vigente.
> Los epitetos, los refranes, los proverbios, los chistes, las
> blasfemias, las injurias, son un catálogo todavía poco estudiado
> pero que salta a la vista – y al oído – como un clamor que incluso
> aturde de tanta agresividad . . . El mundo se define en masculino,
> y el hombre se atribuye la representación de la humanidad
> entera.
>
> (Sau 1981: 219)

Gender in Spanish

We need to be aware when talking about gender that there are different
kinds: biological gender, social gender, and grammatical gender.

■ Find definitions for each of these categories. In what ways are they
fulfilled differently in English and Spanish?

Biological gender is unproblematic, being an objective reality: males are distinguished from females by certain indisputable physiological differences. Social gender is more complicated and refers to behaviour and attributes which are generally regarded as male or female, but may vary in the way they are categorised from society to society, and language community to language community. Finally grammatical gender of course refers to the way words are marked in any given language by categories which we call genders, masculine, feminine, and sometimes neuter. Where problems may arise is in seeing how far these different categories overlap. Grammatical gender does not always coincide with biological and social gender, although there is a tendency to assume it does.

■■ Make a list of words in Spanish which are marked by either masculine or feminine grammatical forms but in fact either uniquely refer to the opposite biological category, or can refer to either sex, or are associated with the opposite social gender. For example, neither '*la persona*' nor '*la gente*' are restricted to describing female people.

When thinking about this exercise you will probably find many names that describe people's professions and trades are masculine, although they can be carried out by either sex. It is normal to talk about '*médico*' regardless of whether the doctor is male or female, and the same has been the case with such words as '*juez*', '*abogado*' and '*ingeniero*'. Look at the following example of how such grammatical/social gender marking might lead to confusion and surprise.

> El profesor estaba esperando a su marido que había de salir de la oficina con el ingeniero de construcción, el cual estaba encinta por tercera vez. Mientras esperaba descubrió al lado del edificio a un campesino que con las manos sucias amamantaba a su bebé. En este momento el profesor pensó en su propio embarazo y en su hijo Manuel, ahora casado con un conocido actor.
>
> (Uwe K. Nissen, cited in García Meseguer 1994: 52)

Whilst this is probably an exceptional, not to say contrived, piece of text, it is grammatically correct, but leaves us trying to work out who is being referred to. Our normal assumptions lead us to expect a masculine noun ('*el profesor*') to have '*una esposa*' rather than '*un marido*'. Of course this teacher is a woman but the masculine title is grammatically correct. In the same way the masculine grammatical form of '*ingeniero*' and '*campesino*' and '*actor*' takes us by surprise. In fact, nowadays we might rightly expect feminine forms of many of these: '*profesora*', '*campesina*' and '*actriz*'.

■■ Through examining contemporary Spanish media, consider to what extent Spanish is changing its grammatical gender of words in response to social changes. Compare this to the trends in the use of *tú* and *usted*.

■■ Using a good monolingual Spanish dictionary, look up some of the words to describe professions mentioned here, or that you have thought of, and see how many still, according to the dictionary, only have a masculine grammatical form.

The choice of the word '*actriz*' versus '*actor*' presents another interesting discussion. When two different forms exist to mark the gender of the person being described as the same thing, do these different words in fact take on distinct meanings? Here social attitudes to the superiority/inferiority of the different sexes' perceived ability to do things may colour the use of the noun.

■ Janet Holmes suggests that in many languages,

> ... [t]he male form is the **unmarked form**, and therefore, it is argued, implicitly the norm. The use of an additional suffix to signal 'femaleness' is seen as conveying the message that women are deviant, abnormal, and not important.
>
> It has also been suggested that suffixes like -*ess* and -*ette* trivialise and diminish women, and when they refer to occupations such as *authoress* and *poetess* carry connotations of lack of seriousness.
>
> (1992: 337–338)

Do you agree with this comment? Does it apply also to Spanish? Do you think there is a difference in Spanish between a pair of nouns like *actor* and *actriz* as opposed to *ingeniero* and *ingeniera*?

In some cases Spanish words (and particularly adjectives) have definitely taken on a completely different meaning according to which sex is being described:

■ Study the following examples taken from García Meseguer (1994: 31):

'Un hombre galante' (atento, obsequioso) frente a 'una mujer galante' (de costumbres licenciosas),

'Un cualquiera' (sin oficio ni beneficio) frente a 'una cualquiera' (mujer de mala vida),

'Un hombre desenvuelto' (de trato agradable, sin timidez) frente a 'una mujer desenvuelta' (coqueta),

'un hombre honrado/honesto' (alude a su actividad en los negocios) frente a 'una mujer honrada/honesta' (alude a su vida sexual).

One of the areas where the form in Spanish seems to point to a sexist focus, discriminating against women, is with the use of the masculine grammatical form in the plural when those being referred to are male and female. A room full of female students with one male student will be addressed as '*vosotros*'. A particularly stark example of this is of course the term which describes the combination of a mother and a father: '*los padres*'.

■ Again changes are beginning to take place to avoid this particular male-dominating situation. Can you think of ways round the masculine plural? Remember that when addressing people you will usually hear '*señores y señoras*'. Why not '*vosotros y vosotras*'? Why do we always place the masculine form before the feminine form even when we do distinguish between the two? Sometimes there are singular collective nouns which can refer to the whole group without simply making a masculine plural form: '*el profesorado*' instead of '*los profesores*', for example (although these words are themselves very often masculine).

Sometimes in Spanish the grammatical gender is only identifiable by the corresponding definite or indefinite article used, with the noun itself ending in a way that is normally associated with a different gender from that of the article. There are various words in Spanish which end in -*a* but are not in fact grammatically feminine. In some cases nor are they necessarily biologically or socially female. For example, the many words ending in -*ista* can usually be either sex when referring to professions (*el/la recepcionista, el/la pianista, el/la dentista, el/la periodista, el/la marxista*, etc.).

Spanish shares with many other languages a further practice which appears to suggest that it is sexist. The common habit of referring to the male person when talking about human kind in general is now well known as being central to the accusations of sexism in language. As in English, French and many other languages, Spanish refers to 'el hombre' when making generalisations about the human race. For example:

> Una nueva teoría evolutiva asegura que el hombre procede del chimpancé pigmeo, y no del común, como se creía ... 'Este estudio es básico para conocer el origen del hombre' dice el doctor Reynolds.
>
> (Cambio 16, 25.III.96)

Depending on how we are meant to interpret this statement, women might be rather glad that they apparently have nothing to do with chimpanzees! This male-centric (and as we can see, often ambiguous) language could be so easily avoided by using words such as '*ser humano*', '*las personas*' or '*los humanos*', for example. In the same way the masculine pronoun 'he' or '*él*' is also used. It is argued that this is a generic form and does not have any specific gender-related meaning, but the fact that it is a grammatically marked form makes this argument unconvincing to many people (particularly women!). By extension, then, the practice of using the male form to describe in the abstract any unspecified person helps reinforce this.

English has grammatical marking only in the pronouns and possessive adjective forms ('he'/'she' and 'his'/'her'), and yet there are many nouns in English in common usage which are in fact gender-specific: chairman, headmaster, postman, actor, being just a few such examples. In fact, although we may at first believe that Spanish will be more easily open to accusations of sexism because of its grammatical gender system, we should remind ourselves that, unlike English, Spanish has a completely unmarked and often ambiguous third-person possessive adjective '*su*' which conceals gender, as well as having the custom of not including subject pronouns on many occasions, thereby also avoiding gender-specificity.

As we have seen, whilst biological gender is easy to identify and grammatical gender can be recognised and learnt, social gender is more complicated and depends on inbuilt and often unconscious beliefs held by society. There are expectations about which gender something 'should' be. This is why we are initially surprised by the text about the teacher waiting for her husband quoted above. These expectations embed sexist language in many of our utterances. They lead to stereotyping in a wide range of written and spoken communications. Job advertisements expect secretaries to be female and miners to be male. School books portray women cooking and looking after children, with men mending cars and using tools. In particular those in positions of power are nearly always unconsciously expected to be men, and this is reflected in linguistic practices.

- Have a look in a good Spanish dictionary for definitions of words that describe activities which are commonly associated with one sex more than the other to see if these stereotypes are confirmed in definitions. First read the definitions found by García Meseguer (1994: 67) in the *Diccionario de la Real Academia Española*.

> BOLO: Almohadilla prolongada y redonda en que *las mujeres* hacen encajes.
> MARTILLO: Herramienta de percusión que usan *los varones* para clavar clavos.

(my emphases)

- Notice the use here of the Spanish word *varón*. Do you see any difference in meaning or function for the two words 'varón' and 'hombre'?

The use of the masculine gender as the unmarked generic form in Spanish is susceptible to social changes. The gender-free language and anti-sexist movements in the English-speaking world have their counterparts in some of the Spanish-speaking world. Once again, the social changes that have taken place in post-Franco Spain have included an awareness of the previously subordinated role of women. Women's movements and pressure have helped improve legal rights for women, reflecting a change in public attitudes which is visible in language use. As we have already noted, there is an increasing use of feminine-marked words for professions; there is also more effort to keep the language of public communications gender-free. In an article reviewing progress and change in the highly bureaucratic language of Spanish public administration between 1982 (when the Socialists first came to power) and 1992, Teresa Tinsley finds many responses to the developments in Spanish society in general. The production of a *Manual de estilo del lenguaje administrativo* has led the way in reforming this archaic and obtuse language. An awareness of the need to make administrative language more gender-free is acknowledged.

> The Spanish Administration has gone further than many institutions in actively promoting strategies which avoid giving the impression that the Administration is *un mundo de varón*. The *Manual* suggests

a variety of tactics to be used in combination: the use of collective nouns such as *el profesorado, el personal funcionario*; the repetition of both masculine and feminine forms where this is possible without becoming too long-winded (e.g. *los trabajadores y las trabajadoras*) or a slash or brackets (*alumno(a)*; *D./Doña*).

(Tinsley 1992: 29)

Tinsley also points out that the Spanish Ministry of Education has published a similar document recommending a sensitivity towards gender-free language, entitled *Recomendaciones para el uso no sexista de la lengua*.

■■■ Examine documents, official forms, and so on published by the Spanish Administration (such as those available at Spanish embassies, or other public places) to see if these directives are in fact being carried out.

■■ Comment on the significance of the Ministry of Education's awareness of the need for changes in this area in the language of its documents.

Gendered language behaviour

Besides analysing the language itself, we should look to see if different language behaviour can be associated with the different sexes. Do women and men speak differently in the same situation? Do they have different attitudes towards the language they use and hear? Is this translated into public language practices? To consider answers to some of these questions you will need to carry out your own fieldwork, by watching Spanish-language television, or listening to the radio, reading Spanish, and above all talking to native speakers.

In order to examine Spanish-language practices, study the features below which are often claimed to be representative of women's language. This list is based loosely on Holmes (1992) and Lakoff (1975). Research in this area has consistently shown that women appear to favour the use of more standard forms and varieties of language. Clearly when making such bold generalisations about women's behaviour, we must acknowledge that it will be affected by such circumstances as social context, group loyalties and communicative purpose. In describing women as subordinate and marginalised, we are not ignoring similar characteristics of other minority or underprivileged groups; nor should we forget that some women are in fact unusually assertive and capable of dominating situations.

■■ Consider some of the following questions:

– Are women more conscious of social status than men? If you believe that they are, might it be because in fact they are aware of their subordinate role in most societies? Do they then (usually unconsciously) compensate by being particularly polite, which normally involves the use of more standard language forms?

– Do women prefer to follow rules and 'correct' models more than men? If so, is this connected with their frequent role-model function for children (as mother and often as teacher)?

Try to decide if your answers are equally true in Spanish-speaking situations which you encounter. Watch TV chat shows and interviews; are men more informal, more colloquial, more blunt than women being interviewed or taking part?

If we agree that this is typical behaviour of women speakers, we are led to the conclusion that it represents a basic lack of confidence and sense of inferiority felt by many women. The other side to this might be a male arrogance and aggressiveness, the two attitudes thereby reinforcing one another. It is argued that this relationship is confirmed in speech behaviour. To appreciate how true this is we should analyse language from the point of view of the tenor aspect of register. What language do women/men typically use when creating relationships? It is often claimed that women display more hesitation, on the one hand, and more need to convince and thus emphasise their speech on the other.

■■ Analyse a piece of transcribed dialogue in Spanish to see how far this is true. Do women use more tag questions; more 'fillers'; more intensifiers (like the -*ísimo* ending) or extensive modifiers compared to men? Do men use more swearing and affirmative statements than women? Do men interrupt more than women?

If it is true that women tend to prefer more standard forms of language, it seems reasonable to expect that this attitude to language will also extend to their choice of language in multilingual situations. In the context of multilingual communities in the Spanish-speaking world it is important to test this out. The implications are far-reaching for Language Planning (see Chapter 10) and particularly for the education system (see Chapter 11), as well as for those using communication to persuade, influence and inform, i.e. the media and advertising.

■■ Study and discuss these examples of where the choice of language learnt and used was determined by women.

1   Archer and Costello (1990) report how in the outskirts of La Paz the Aymara-speaking immigrant population are participating in literacy and adult education classes. These are almost solely attended by women, and in fact one organisation, the CDA, is uniquely for women. One of the dilemmas was in which language to give the literacy classes. Many attempts had been made to teach through the mother tongue, Aymara, but this had often proved unsuccessful. The women rejected literacy in Aymara as they did not accord it the same status in the urban life they had migrated to. As one of the literacy workers says:

The women want Spanish . . . every time that we ask them they always say that they want Spanish. The women are adults, they won't lose their own language . . . Cultural values are given within the family, and have lasted generations . . . These values will not be lost easily, but they are more likely to be lost if the women cannot stand up for themselves and assert their rights . . . in Spanish.

(Margarita Callisaya, cited in Archer and Costello 1990: 167)

2   In Galicia, unlike in other minority linguistic communities in Spain, the local language does not enjoy particularly high prestige. Whilst it is widely spoken (see Chapter 10) this is because it is the mother tongue of a rural, traditional society. Most people speak Galician at home, but when children go to school and then to look for jobs, often in urban areas, Castilian is considered the correct form of speech and is associated with status and success. During the years after the Civil War and up until quite recently this attitude was above all the view of Galician women. Galicia became at that time a society with a large predominance of women as many of the men migrated to northern

Europe in search of jobs and wages to send home. Social attitudes, then, were more than usually instilled by a matriarchal society which consistently and overwhelmingly favoured Castilian and was ashamed of Galician.

As we saw in Chapter 7, how the media uses language is a useful social barometer. We would expect then that the media would both reflect society's attitudes to gender, including sexist stereotypes where these exist, and/or the movements to eradicate these when they are taking place.

■■ Compile data on the participation of women in the media, and especially television. Compare their role on English-speaking and Spanish-speaking TV. For example, how often do women appear as the experts asked to comment on news stories? What is the proportion of reporters and interviewers who are women? How many chat shows and 'mesas redondas' are conducted by women? Are men given the same 'adorning' roles that women so often perform (e.g. holding the props in TV shows)? Do women speak as often as men, and what subjects do they talk about?

Attempts have been made to involve more women in the media, especially in such roles as newsreader, weather forecast presenter, show hosts, and so on, responding to changing social attitudes in general. Nonetheless, as late as 1988, a survey showed that in the European Community only fifteen per cent of television personnel was female (*Cambio 16* 24.X.88).

On the whole the media seems to confirm negative and inferior images of women, and their participation is in subordinate roles. In some circumstances, however, women have been able to take advantage of the power of the media as a form of communication as they develop their linguistic awareness. We have already noted (in Chapter 7, and see also Chapter 11) that 'radioliteracy' has been used as a way of raising the prestige of indigenous communities and their languages in places such as Guatemala and Bolivia. In Chile too, marginalised women in poor urban areas of Santiago were encouraged to develop literacy skills which they soon adapted to use on radio and television as a way of empowering and liberating themselves (Archer and Costello 1990; Boyle in Radcliffe and Westwood 1993). In these experiences women learnt to use the language of public life, of wider communication, information and persuasion.

In the area of advertising, language and imagery still normally place women in an inferior role. Frequently in Spanish advertisements women are 'displayed' in provocative or decorative support roles (to sell a car, or cook the new food product, or wash with the best washing power) but often do not actually say much. In one Spanish TV advertisement various electrodomestic products are demonstrated by a woman (an iron, an electric milk warmer, a vacuum cleaner) with a man's voice providing the voice-over. In another advertisement a man dressed in a smart suit is shown spraying highly polished furniture with a new cleaner in a situation it is hard to imagine he has ever experienced. Women wait at home for their husbands to return from work and then give them masculine presents. Even in an advertisement which refers to the '*nueva mujer juvenil*' the protagonist, wearing a short skirt, walking assertively, and selling perfume, appears in the role of office girl/secretary. The text of the following advertisement for a photocopier is particularly revealing of continuing sexism in advertising:

> Su función en la oficina es hacer copias ¡Y cuántas y qué bien las hace! ¡Y qué baratas! ¡Y nunca se equivoca! Aunque es muy jovencita tiene una gran experiencia, está trabajando a pleno rendimiento en millares de oficinas y despachos en todo el mundo. (Ya ha conquistado a notarios, abogados, gestores administrativos . . . etc, etc, etc.) . . .
>
> Es una colaboradora modelo, jamás protesta, no precisa Seguros Sociales ni cobra horas extras . . . ¡Trabaja toda la vida por el sueldo de un mes! Compruébelo, llámenos por teléfono y tendremos mucho gusto en hacerle una demostración.
>
> (Hickey 1977: 52)

■ Notice how the grammatical gender of the product – '*la máquina*' – allows the play on words to be effected. Comment on the sexist language and innuendo used in this advertisement. The 'upgrading' of the machine to an animate being, and one that is compared favourably to the normal female performing the same role, is used to appeal to the potential buyer's perception of the role (and efficiency, cooperativeness, etc.) of women and this contrast is used with the intention of being humorous.

In March 1994 *Televisión Española* broadcast a chat show dedicated to the theme of '*La Mujer y el Hombre en el Lenguaje*' (note the order of the sexes). The four invited participants were Ana Mañeru, '*directora*' (according to TVE) of the education programme for the Instituto de la

Mujer; Mercedes Mediavilla, 'profesora' (according to TVE) de la lengua; Gregorio Salvador, member of the Real Academia Española; and the writer (see above) Alvaró García Meseguer. At the end of the programme they were each asked to give their opinion on three specific suggestions made in a pamphlet being circulated, which aimed to upgrade the role of women by making deliberate changes in social language behaviour. The three points were:

- En vez de usar 'el hombre' emplear 'los hombres y las mujeres';
- Evitar la asimetría en el tratamiento, específicamente el uso del artículo definido antes de la mujer pero no antes del hombre ('la Thatcher' pero no 'el Chirac');
- Feminizar los cargos, carreras, puestos, etc.

■ Given the information you have about these four people, what do you think their answers might be? What factors lead you to your conclusions?

■■ Do you think four similar Chileans or Venezuelans would answer in the same way? Can you think of similar changes which might be made to remove sexism from English?

The participants' responses mostly supported the three suggestions. Gregorio Salvador did not believe there was any asymmetry in the way the two sexes were addressed. He also felt that the use of the masculine plural as a generic term was 'un hecho de la lengua, y ya está'. It emerged that Ana Mañeru was in fact the author of the pamphlet and so obviously agreed with it! She made the point that she believed that society should be aiming to remove the sharp division between the sexes which set up a hierarchy of men over women, and that anything, including language change, which helped this was to be welcomed. Alvaro García Meseguer was almost entirely supportive of the suggested changes. He felt that the extent to which people chose feminine forms for things like professions, should be optional and dependent on circumstances (for example, notice the use of 'author' rather than 'authoress' in this paragraph!). He favoured the use of 'varón' rather than 'hombre' as a way of avoiding the ambiguity of masculine gender versus generic form. Mercedes Mediavilla supported all three changes, but pointed out that even the use of, for example, 'hombres y mujeres' maintained the hierarchical order of men above women.

Throughout the programme all four participants stressed a point which has emerged throughout this chapter, which is that language in itself is not sexist – be it English, Spanish or whichever – but that it is the attitudes and behaviour of its users which certainly is, reflecting sexist views held by society in general.

Further reading

For general introductions to some of the ideas discussed in this chapter, see Lakoff (1975) and Holmes (1992). An interesting and provocative collection of essays on the subject of language and gender which develops the point that women share similar characteristics with other marginalised groups is the *International Journal of the Sociology of Language*, 94, 1992, edited by Tove Bull and Toril Swan. For a very wide-ranging and interesting discussion of the Spanish language (mainly from the viewpoint of Spain), see García Meseguer (1994).

● ● ●

Part three

Current issues:
language as national
identity marker

Language policies
in post-Franco Spain

Chapter 9

I N   T H E   C H A P T E R S   O F   P A R T   T H R E E we will be looking at the present situation of Spanish throughout the world in terms of its social and political significance. On the one hand, in Spain, the death of Franco and the end of his dictatorial regime have led to radical changes in Spanish society closely reflected in language policies, including a far greater recognition of and tolerance towards the linguistic minorities. On the other, the increase in Spanish speakers world-wide continues apace, to a large degree as a result of the high birth rate amongst the Spanish-speaking populations of the Americas. We will see how this is becoming a particularly interesting phenomenon in the USA, as well as examining how it affects language planning in Latin America.

The 1978 Spanish Constitution

In this chapter we will start by examining the huge changes that have taken place in post-Franco Spain. Central to these changes is the implementation of a new constitution in 1978. Not only are the language policies enshrined in this document of interest to us, but so too is the very language in which it is couched, a superb example of the language of compromise and consensus, of ambiguity and interpretation.

Artículo 2

La Constitución se fundamenta en la indisoluble unidad de la Nación española, patria común e indivisible de todos los españoles, y reconoce y garantiza el derecho a la autonomía de las nacionalidades y regiones que la integran y la solidaridad entre todas ellas.

■ What do you think are meant here by the words 'nación' and 'nacionalidad'? Do you think they mean the same in their literal English translation? What about the word 'autonomía' – we tend to think of this as meaning something very close to 'independence' in

English. Is there a better English word to describe the Spanish concept?

■ Notice how the juxtaposition of words like *'unidad'*, *'indisoluble'*, *'indivisible'* and *'solidaridad'* with words such as *'autonomía'*, and *'nacionalidades'* or *'regiones'* in the plural constitutes a deliberate attempt to please everyone. This is a fine line to tread and is being constantly challenged by contemporary Spanish politics.

As a result of the new constitution Spain is now divided politically into seventeen *Comunidades Autónomas*, all with significant delegated powers. The Catalans, Basques and Galicians were the first, as so-called *regiones históricas*, to receive their Statutes of Autonomy in the late seventies and early eighties, but eventually the entire country was organised along these lines. Although, compared to earlier historical periods, the situation in terms of regional recognition by central government is vastly improved, the relationship between central government and the autonomous regions continues on occasion to be uneasy. At times this has in fact strengthened the position of the more assertive regional governments, who have found themselves being wooed by minority government parties in Madrid. Both the socialist government of Felipe González in 1993 and the right-wing Partido Popular government of José María Aznar in 1996 relied on the support of the Catalans, and to a lesser extent, the Basques, in order to stay in power. The concessions sought in return for this support were, amongst others, fiscal, legal and, in the case of the Catalans, even linguistic.

Article 3 of the post-Franco Constitution

Of particular interest to the discussion of the current sociolinguistic situation in Spain is Article 3 of this constitution. This is the first time that a Spanish constitution has engaged to such a full extent with the linguistic rights of Spanish citizens. The article reads:

Artículo 3

1   El castellano es la lengua oficial del Estado. Todos los españoles tienen el deber de conocerla y el derecho a usarla.

2 Las demás lenguas españolas serán también oficiales en las respectivas Comunidades Autónomas de acuerdo con sus Estatutos.

3 La riqueza de las distintas modalidades lingüísticas de España es un patrimonio cultural que será objeto de especial respeto y protección.

■ Consider the first sentence of Clause 1. Why is it so significant that Spain's official language is called 'castellano' and not 'español'?

Both here and in the next clause it is clear that the constitution implies that there is more than one 'lengua española'. In the Franco era, 'Castilian' *was* 'Spanish' and it would have been unthinkable to specify the former. With the publication of this clause came strong opposition to the term 'Castilian' from various quarters, and not just from those who had supported the Franco regime. These critics object to the notion that the term *lengua española* could be used in the plural. Gregorio Salvador, an outspoken linguist and member of the Real Academia Española, commenting on the first and second clauses, writes:

> Lenguas de España llamo a las que, con notable impropiedad, designa el artículo tercero de la Constitución como 'lenguas españolas', en una redacción chapucera donde se ignora que el adjetivo *española* aplicada a *lengua* constituye una lexia compleja con valor unitario que, por tradición y por uso, sólo quiere decir una cosa: 'lengua castellana'.
>
> (Salvador 1987: 92)

In another article Salvador has argued:

> ... el idioma llamado allí *castellano* es *español* para la mayor parte de sus hablantes, es *español* en casi todas las Constituciones americanas ... Y es *español* o *lengua española* en todos los países extranjeros, ese es su nombre universal ... [E]sa lengua no es sólo patrimonio español, sino de muchos otros pueblos, y ... los españoles sólo alcanzamos ya a ser la novena parte de sus usuarios.
>
> (Salvador 1992: 111–112)

■ Even allowing for the fact that there do exist significant groups in Latin America who in fact prefer to use the term *castellano*, is this comment about the universality of the term *español* a fair one?

Notice also how in Article 2 the '*Nación española*' is referred to, but here in Article 3, in the context of the official language, Spain is called the '*Estado*'. Perhaps the political boundaries of a state are more easily defined, for the legal purposes of implementing an official language, than those of a nation.

This clause, however, goes on to say that all Spaniards have a *duty* to know Castilian. Immediately the radical tone of the first sentence is counterbalanced by the prescriptive directive of the second. It is difficult to find anywhere else in the world a national constitution which prescribes the *duty* to know a language.

- However, what is meant by 'know'? Remember, in particular, that the Spanish word is '*conocer*' which implies the English idea of 'to be acquainted with' rather than '*saber hablar*' which has the English idea of 'know how to speak'. Is it something purely passive requiring no active competence? How can it be demonstrated that a citizen does or does not 'know' a language?

This directive to know Castilian is highly ambiguous and is constantly being tested for legal interpretation and clarification. For example, the Spanish daily *El País* reported the President of the Tribunal Constitucional, Miguel Rodriguez-Piñero as claiming that the Tribunal

> ... ha dicho ... que el deber de conocer el castellano quiere decir que su desconocimiento no exime a nadie de hacer algo, pero sin que ello suponga una coacción a nadie.
>
> (*El País* 23.II.94)

Clause 2 is particularly interesting to examine, not only for what it tells us about changes in the way the Spanish state regards its linguistic minorities, but for its relevance to the broader discussions about two important **principles** of language rights legislation, those of **personality** and of **territoriality**.

- ■ The first question posed by Clause 2 is what is meant by '*las demás lenguas españolas*'? Leaving aside the highly contentious debate as to whether there can be more than one '*lengua española*', we are still left to decide which languages might become official in their Autonomous Communities. How would you decide this? What criteria would you use (remember the definitions you formulated in

Chapter 1 for language and dialect)? Could the definition of these languages vary over time and circumstance?

The working definition has generally been to recognise the languages in which the Constitution has been published as being those regarded as '*las demás lenguas*'. However, this has had some strange consequences. The Valencians, who have been keen to establish their different identity from the Catalans, insisted that there should be a Valencian version of the 1978 Constitution. This was granted, with the result that a document was published which, almost without exception, was word for word identical to the Catalan version!

■■ Discuss the significance of this example. Why would the Valencians want to stress their difference from the Catalans? From a historical and linguistic perspective would you want to call Valencian a 'language' or a 'dialect'? Explain the reasons for your decision. As another variety clearly closely related to Catalan, where does this situation leave the linguistic form spoken in the Balearic Islands?

Table 9.1 shows the Autonomous Communities who, as a result of the Constitution, have declared the language of their community as their '*lengua propia*', with the name they call this language and the number of its speakers.

TABLE 9.1 Autonomous Communities with their own language. Name of own language and population

Comunidades Autónomas con lengua propia	Denominación de la lengua	Población	
		No. de habitantes (*)	% sobre población española
Cataluña	catalán	6.115.579	15,50
Valencia	valenciano	3.923.841	9,95
I. Baleares	catalán	745.944	1,89
Galicia	gallego	2.720.445	6,89
País Vasco	euskera	2.109.009	5,34
Navarra	vascongado	523.563	1,32

(*) Fuente: Población de hecho al 1 de marzo de 1991. Censo de Población de 1991 (INE).

Source: Centro de Investigaciones Sociológicas 1994: 10

■ Discuss this concept of *'lengua propia'* which is a term that has been invented for the Spanish situation and intends to distinguish this status from either 'official' or 'national'.

Clause 2 also grants the Territoriality Principle to the minority language communities. This principle recognises a particular language's right to be the dominant/official language in a specified territory, for whoever resides in this territory. However, Clause 1 has already proclaimed the Personality Principle for speakers of Castilian. This principle acknowledges an individual's right to speak their language wherever they reside within the constitution's jurisdiction, i.e. all of Spain. These two clauses are therefore inevitably in conflict. The clear geographical limitation placed on the minority languages means realistically that their future role will always take second place to Castilian.

■■ Is the intention of Article 3, in giving preference to Castilian, through the Personality Principle, compatible with Article 14 of the Constitution guaranteeing equality to all Spanish citizens?

Artículo 14

Los españoles son iguales ante la ley, sin que pueda prevalecer discriminación alguna por razón de nacimiento, raza, sexo, religión, o cualquier otra condición o circunstancia personal o social.

Those Spanish citizens whose mother tongue is not Castilian could argue that they do not have equal linguistic rights to those who are Castilian mother-tongue speakers. A native Catalan speaker cannot insist on the right to use Catalan in official contexts in, for example, Madrid. Native Basque speakers cannot expect the Spanish state to provide Basque teaching to their children if they happen to live in, for example, Seville. On the other hand, throughout the Spanish state, Castilian may be used and must be provided for.

What seems a well-intentioned policy to promote linguistic pluralism may in fact, consciously or otherwise, create linguistic enclaves and support the subordination of the peripheries to the Castilian core. However, as if to counter the potential negative sense of the second clause, the third one does seem to confirm a belief in linguistic pluralism.

- How strong a commitment do you think this clause expresses to linguistic pluralism? What do you think is meant by '*respeto*' and '*protección*'? Can they have any effect unless the resources to back them up are guaranteed?

It can certainly be argued that this third clause has opened the way in parts of Spain for more radical ways of seeing the relationship between language and identity. It allows Autonomous Communities to define their local linguistic variety, and even when this is not considered a separate language from Castilian, its own particular features can be recognised and protected. This has inspired work on lexical and phonological features in, for example, Andalusia and the Canary Islands in order to draw up guidelines on what constitutes these regions' respective language varieties.

- In what linguistic **domains** do you think this attention to the local varieties can have an effect on public use? Notice, for example, that in the Canary Islands the Ministry of Education has published a list of the most usual words of Canary Spanish. Where would it be relevant to use such a list?

Although ambiguities obviously do exist in the new constitutional framework regarding language policy, there is no denying the substantial advances that have taken place since 1978 in the promotion and status of Spain's minority languages, as we shall see in the next chapter. However, by limiting the promotion of non-Castilian languages to discrete geographical areas, the continued domination of Castilian as 'national' language is ensured. The minorities' cultural identities are only acknowledged when they are linked to territorial identities.

The other minority languages of Spain

The linguistic map of Spain needs to be analysed with two other elements in mind: the role of ever-increasing groups of immigrants; and the effect of a more closely integrated European Union.

Until now we have only referred to the indigenous languages of the Iberian Peninsula when discussing minority language communities in Spain. However, there is a growing and significant number of non-European immigrants now resident in the European Union, many of whom do not speak as their mother tongue the language of any member-state. Spain has only recently begun to experience the social and cultural effects of such immigration, largely with groups from North Africa and Latin America. For many years Latin Americans have come to Spain, sometimes in search of a better economic situation and in search of employment, sometimes as political refugees. Even during the Franco years there were many Latin American visitors. Some of these stayed, and many more have come since the return of democracy. These Latin Americans come from all over the continent, and should not, of course, be lumped together as if they were a homogeneous group. Some are white middle class students and professionals seeking further educational qualifications and experience. Many are from poorer groups in search of employment and better social opportunities. Many of these are easily recognised by their physical characteristics and are often black or from Latin American indigenous groups. In Spain, a country which is largely European in its racial features, this is leading to an alarming increase in racism.

However, what most of these immigrants and visitors have in common with the majority of Spain's population is a shared language – albeit with important differences in accent, vocabulary and usage. Along with a sense of shared cultures and religion, the knowledge that Spanish will be the language of communication is paramount in attracting these people to Spain.

Besides this group of immigrants, there is also a rapidly growing group of immigrants from North Africa, many of whom arrive illegally in Spain, often en route to other parts of Europe. The majority of these are of Arab racial features, and are Muslims. They do not of course speak Spanish. They are perceived as very different from the rest of the Spanish population (despite the shared historical past with part, at least, of Spain). Intolerance of difference and fear of competition for jobs, housing, and so on is often particularly provoked by the inability to speak Spanish and to communicate easily.

■■ Given that immigrant groups usually cluster together and concentrate in areas round large towns and cities where jobs might be available, this new immigration often lives side by side with internal migrant groups from other parts of Spain. What are some of the problems you would expect to associate with this social phenomenon in places such as Barcelona and Madrid?

A further minority group who often get forgotten is the gypsy community. Particularly in southern Spain, this is a significant minority community. Whilst the gypsies have lived for centuries in Spain, they remain in many ways marginalised from mainstream society, by their cultural customs, traditions, and to a lesser extent, linguistic habits. *Caló*, which is the name given the linguistic variety spoken by Spanish (and Portuguese) gypsies, is best described as a dialect of Spanish, with many different words and expressions, but with a recognisable Castilian base.

■ Apart from racist prejudices towards the gypsies which manifestly do exist in Spain, can you think of ways in which their language might present particular difficulties? Consider in particular the implications for the education of gypsy children.

Spanish language policies and the European Union

In 1986 Spain joined the European Community. Such membership of international organisations had been first refused and then only grudgingly granted by some bodies during the Franco years. EC membership, then, was considered by many Spaniards as the final stamp of approval by the international community on their country's new democratic system. However, being part of this supra-national organisation means that Spain, like the other member-states, must consider how far she will have to integrate with her fellow members, economically, socially, politically, and even linguistically. The present EU policies and directives on language affect Spain in different ways:

1   Spanish became an official working language of the EU once Spain joined, in common with the official languages of all the other member-states (except for Irish and Luxembourgish).

■■ How important is this for Spanish as a world language? Discuss this status in the context of Castilian's already privileged position as protected by Article 3, Clause 1 of the 1978 Spanish Constitution.

2   The EU has issued various directives about the teaching of languages, and the teaching of people's mother tongues (see also Chapter 11).

■■ What are the implications for Spain if it is to honour the spirit of the EC's 1977 directive encouraging all member-states to provide at least some mother tongue education for the children of immigrants? How might the provision of services in the minority languages bring into conflict those communities who speak *indigenous* minority languages as opposed to those who speak *immigrant* languages? Is this a tension found in other parts of Europe? (See, for example, Coulmas 1991 to help you in answering this.)

3   The third influence of EU language policy is from the community's support for minority and regional languages, which are carefully called 'lesser-used languages' in the EU. These are backed by EU resources such as regional aid and initiatives like those pursued by the European Bureau for Lesser-Used Languages and the Mercator Project. Both of these aim to improve knowledge and research about Europe's minority languages, to sponsor the teaching and learning of these languages, and foster good relations between those groups using them.

■■ Discuss ways in which these initiatives coincide with Article 3 of Spain's new Constitution.

There are many commentators who argue that changes in political power structures within the EU may point to the emergence of a 'Europe of the Regions', where the traditional national state centre will be increasingly bypassed through a relationship between the European supranational centres of power and the local regional centres. This is viewed by Catalans, Basques and Galicians as a real possibility for the strengthening of their particular cultures and languages. Moreover, a major premise of the European Community is the encouragement of and right to freedom of movement of persons within and across the member-states.

■■ What are the language implications of such a policy that challenge the traditional view of language tied to a particular cultural and geographical space?

As has been seen in the discussion in this chapter, language policies and their implementation have been radically changed since the death of Franco, with the introduction of a democratic system, the enacting of a new constitution and Spanish membership of the European Community. These changes are not without their problems. Much of the consensus and the desire and enthusiasm to 'make things work' of the early post-Franco days have now disappeared. Spain shares with many of her neighbours many social problems, such as economic recession, unemployment and unrealised aspirations from an educated and impatient population. In the next chapter we will see (amongst other issues) how far language policies have influenced linguistic and social patterns in the minority linguistic communities of Spain.

■■■ Having discussed the legal framework for current Spanish language policies in detail, now analyse other national constitutions, for example the Mexican one. Are language rights treated in a similar way? Is the language as ambiguous and in need of judicial interpretation as that which is used in the case of the Spanish document?

Further reading

For provocative discussions of the 1978 Constitution and Article 3, see Salvador (1987; 1992). Bastardas and Boix (1994) contain useful chapters on the legal framework and its implementation, as does also Mar-Molinero (1990). For discussions of the Principle of Territoriality, and in particular how it applies to Spain, see Bastardas and Boix (1994) and Mar-Molinero and Stevenson (1991). For gypsies in Spain see Cebrián Abellán (1992). For a good overview of the issues involved in language policies in the European Union see the edited collection by Florian Coulmas (1991), and an interesting historical survey right up to the current time, Siguan (1996).

•   •   •

Language planning

A S WE HAVE SEEN IN PART ONE and the last chapter, national constitutions and laws will often enshrine a government's desired language policies, opening the way for state and private organisations to implement them. The framework into which much of this work fits is that of **language planning (LP)**, a form of social planning that has become more overt and consciously organised in the last twenty to thirty years. Whilst some planning of language use has always been undertaken by governments and others wishing to influence linguistic outcomes, its organisation into a very structured and systematic branch of social planning has largely coincided with the need to plan for the development of official/national languages in post-colonial contexts in the latter half of the twentieth century.

A synthesis of the growing literature on language planning leads us to suggest the following definition:

> *Language planning aims deliberately and consciously to influence or change individual and/or societal language behaviour.*

■■ As a result of this definition, who do you think carries out language planning? To answer this, think about examples of major linguistic behavioural change. For example, find out who proposed, promoted and resourced the change of written script at the beginning of this century in Turkey. Which groups support the use of gender-free language, or so-called 'politically correct' language? What would the word 'subsidiarity' have meant to the average British citizen until the 1990s? Who has been responsible for widely proclaiming a particular meaning for this word since then?

In summary we can say that language planning is implemented by Governments (whose policies are usually being activated in the first place) and government agencies (such as the education system); by supra-national groups (such as international agencies and transnational business); or by individual and non-institutional organisations (such as pressure groups, folk societies, the media, religious groups). Since to some extent the success of the project will depend on resources, we may believe that the last category will only succeed if they persuade institutions or governments to back their campaigns.

■■ Can you think of examples from the discussions in this book for each of the above categories which have influenced the use of either Spanish or the minority languages spoken in Spanish-speaking areas?

Language planning has usually been divided into two principal categories, which are **corpus planning** and **status planning**. A further category has been recently added to this of **acquisition planning** (Cooper 1989). All three of these apply to the current Spanish situation, as we shall see.

■ Corpus planning deals with the internal organisation of the language, its corpus. What aspects will this focus on? Who do you think will be responsible for it?

One of the earliest influences on the corpus planning of Spanish was carried out by King Alfonso X, as we have seen, and the various national language academies are also central in this activity.

While corpus planning looks at the codification and elaboration of the language, status planning seeks to promote the role of a selected language or language variety by increasing its use, influencing attitudes to it and supporting it with resources.

■■ In which aspects of public language do you think it will be crucial to use the targeted language to achieve its promotion? In places you have visited think about what has made you aware that you are in a multilingual society, or one where a lesser-used language is being promoted. (This may be Wales, or Belgium, or Catalonia, or Florida, for example!)

Acquisition planning in a sense develops status planning by identifying more clearly the ways in which the language use will be expanded, such as through the education system. One could say that whereas status planning focuses on the way society thinks about the language, acquisition planning focuses on how it is learnt.

Another important term has become significant in the context of current language planning in Spain, and that is the term **normalisation**. All the present language legislation in Spain refers to linguistic normalisation, but the meaning of this term is somewhat ambiguous. It seems that the word was originally borrowed by Spanish commentators from the literal translation of the French where it was used to mean 'standardisation'. Over the years, beginning with various Catalan sociolinguists in the seventies, the word has come to encompass far more than simply linguistic standardisation, the latter being confined to only the corpus planning part of language planning. Normalisation seeks to make a language 'normal', i.e. to enable it to be used in all normal linguistic functions. It may also refer to attempts to return it to its 'normal' role, often interpreted as being the status and role of the minority languages before the Franco regime. Immediately preceding the dictatorship minority languages had enjoyed the high prestige accorded them during the Second Republic. To some commentators this situation represents their 'normal' role in society and is the one which should be re-introduced. At the very least the aim is to lift minority languages from their status of subordinate language, and to allow them to be considered equal and, therefore, normal.

Language planning in contemporary Spain

With the introduction of Article 3 of the 1978 Spanish Constitution the way was open for considerable work to take place in the deliberate promotion and revival of Spain's minority languages. The ultimate objective of all the language planners of minority languages in Spain is to promote their language to equal status with Castilian and thereby create equal stable bilingualism. To do this they seek to 'normalise' their language, in whatever ways considered necessary. Apart from any intrinsic interest in examining the Spanish linguistic minorities' success or otherwise, this language-planning project has attracted wider interest as an example of LP aims which accept minority status and seek to accommodate the language alongside the undisputed majority language. So often in LP situations a linguistic variety is being promoted in preference to and in order to replace and demote another language or variety. Clearly the objectives and programmes for these two contrasting situations will be different, and this is why the Spanish context is being keenly watched.

After the passing of the 1978 Constitution in Spain the three 'historic' regions of Catalonia, Euskadi (the Basque Country) and Galicia experienced the greatest activity in terms of LP efforts. These efforts are supported not only by Article 3 of the Constitution but also by the relevant Autonomy Statutes which were subsequently passed to set up each *Comunidad Autónoma*, and, in particular, by the local Linguistic Normalisation Laws. All three of the so-called historic regions passed these linguistic laws, as a direct response to the second clause of Article 3 which encourages recognition of local languages '*de acuerdo con sus Estatutos*'. There are many similarities between the Autonomous Communities as regards this legal framework and the areas of linguistic activity through which language planning is being pursued, but there are also important differences, as should be expected when recognising that the various Autonomous Communities are not homogeneous and display marked differences.

Catalonia

The most active and successful language promotion programmes are taking place in Catalonia.

■■ Why should this fact not surprise us? To answer this, find out the relative sizes of the populations of the three Autonomous Communities, and consider their economic situations. Also refer back to their historical developments described in Chapter 3.

The Autonomous Community of Catalonia has more than six million inhabitants. As in the Basque Country and Galicia the local government has set up a Directorate to coordinate language promotion programmes. This includes: encouraging both the teaching of Catalan and teaching through the medium of Catalan (see Chapter 11); the development of modern terminologies in Catalan; the use of the local language in all government, administrative and official public use, as well as in the media. The results are spectacular: the rise in the number of schools offering some or much of their curricula in Catalan is sharp; most public notices, street names, menus, bank cheques, entrance tickets, and so on are in Catalan (sometimes exclusively, sometimes bilingually). There are Barcelona and Gerona daily papers in Catalan, television channels either uniquely transmitting in Catalan or giving some programmes in Catalan, there are also numerous Catalan local radio stations. Theatre, cinema and written publications flourish in Catalan. Significantly, much of this includes translations from languages other than Castilian.

Catalan has always been the language of all the Catalan population, including, significantly, the upper and middle classes.

■■ Compare this situation with other sociolinguistic contexts, including the Basque and Galician ones, where a minority language exists. This exceptional prestige for Catalan marks it out in sociolinguistic terms, and points to the need for caution when attempting to draw any wider implications from the Catalan experience.

This has meant that the language can serve as a symbol of social mobility and acceptance, with the ensuing favourable attitudes to its use and teaching. This has undoubtedly helped overcome its single greatest obstacle which is the large non-native Catalan-speaking immigrant population now found resident in Catalonia. Almost 50 per cent of Catalonia's population was not born there, largely the result of the huge influx of migrant workers which Catalonia, like various other northern industrialised areas, experienced in the decades after the Civil War. Many of these came from poor rural Andalusian regions, although a sizeable population also came from Galicia.

■■ What kind of effect would this large influx of non-Catalan speakers have on the use of Catalan? Note that migration usually tends to concentrate in focal areas, for example, in the industrial belt of Greater Barcelona. What additional challenges does this present the language planners? Remember, also, that much of this immigration took place precisely at a time when the Franco regime was rigorously proscribing the use and teaching of Catalan.

However, unlike Basque, but like Galician, Catalan's accessibility to Castilian speakers, as another related Romance language, has helped provide a very high incidence of passive knowledge of the language by the region's population.

Like many other minority languages, Catalan does, however, share with Basque and Galician, albeit to a lesser degree, the challenge of mass communications in modern technological societies.

■■ What are the technological advances of the late twentieth century which help create the so-called 'global village', and which thus strengthen the role and dominance of certain major world languages?

Euskadi (the Basque Country)

With less than two and a half million inhabitants the Basque community is the smallest of the three where a minority language is being promoted. Fewer than 25 per cent of these claim to speak Basque, reflecting the difficulty of access to this language which, unlike Catalan, Galician and Castilian, is not part of the Romance language continuum. The language has considerably less prestige and status than Catalan within its community, although during the sixties and seventies it was given a certain boost by being a symbol of the nationalist movement ETA. Another development, dating back to the sixties, was the introduction of Basque schools, teaching Basque and providing a curriculum through the Basque medium. These schools are known as '*ikastolas*' and were an important attempt to promote Basque identity, originally as largely clandestine groups, and then increasingly throughout the sixties and seventies, as private organisations, often working as non-profit-making parent cooperatives. However, there is no strong literary tradition in Basque, and the codification of the language and selection of a standard variety from various competing dialects is very recent. All of this has made the teaching of Basque and its use in public life very much more difficult. The Basque Country also has an important non-Basque immigrant population who have been slow to want to learn Basque, which, unlike Catalan, has been associated with rural areas and backward traditionalism. There have, nonetheless, been improvements and successes as Basque is promoted through the education system (there are now state-funded *ikastolas*), and used in local government wherever possible. But the obstacles against the learning of Basque create the sense that its promotion is above all symbolic rather than practical.

■■ Compare Basque with other languages which appear to be largely symbolic markers rather than widely-used forms of communication. Is the Irish situation, for example, similar (see, for example, Fasold 1984)? Discuss whether in the long run a language can exist if it only performs the symbolic but not the communicative functions.

Galicia

Galicia like the Basque Country contains a small population, but by way of contrast has not been affected by immigration. Therefore a very high percentage speak the language, some 90 per cent of its nearly three million population. However, Galician lacks status and therefore is not used for social advancement or for more educated literate purposes, except by a tiny minority of middle-class intellectuals. Galician language-planning activities, similar in conception to the Catalan and Basque ones, are attempting to counter these attitudes. However, an important difference in the case of Galician is the existence of a society which has known heavy emigration, leading in general terms to a conservative 'holding' mentality, particularly with womenfolk waiting for the return of the perceived head of the family.

■■   Minority communities are often in fact associated with very conservative lifestyles. They are frequently criticised for being backward-looking, clinging to the past and not wanting change. Compare the Catalans with this stereotype. Do you think that Galicia fits this image? It must be emphasised in this context that Castilian has always been seen as the 'acceptable' language for children to be taught, and for public communication. To promote Galician above Castilian is viewed as a radical, and largely unwanted, change.

Such a predominantly rural society has not encouraged belief in cultural independence and confidence. Moreover, whatever changes are now taking place as a result of the new language policies must also be seen in the context of a counter movement by the so-called 'Reintegrationists', a small but vociferous group who want closer links with Portugal and Portuguese, which they see as the rightful home of Galician. Neither the reintegrationists nor the isolationists (those who see Galician culture and language as separate from either of their larger neighbours) are able to substantially counter the influence and dominance of Castilian.

Evaluating language planning in Spain

An important aspect of language planning is its continuous evaluation. The introduction of language censuses and frequent language use surveys are part of the way the Spanish Autonomous Communities monitor the success or failure of their normalisation programmes.

Table 10.1, which compares census data from 1986 for Catalan and Basque and for 1991 for Galician with a survey carried out in 1993, shows

TABLE 10.1 A comparison of census and survey data on the use of community languages

	Catalán (Cataluña)	Valenciano (Valencia)	Catalán (I. Baleares)	Gallego (Galicia)	Euskera (P. Vasco)	Euskera (Navarra)
Habla:						
Censo	64	57	79	91	25	10
Encuesta	74	55	71	88	31	10
Sólo entiende:						
Censo	26	17	10	6	18	5
Encuesta	22	35	23	10	15	8
No entiende:						
Censo	10	26	11	3	57	85
Encuesta	4	10	6	1	53	82

Source: Centro de Investigaciones Sociológicas 1994: 14

improvements in language knowledge for Catalan and Basque, but a slight decrease for Galician. This would seem to accord with the description of language-planning activities described above. The success in terms of increased users is greatest for Catalan, where the LP is most vigorous and widely accepted.

TABLE 10.2 Language attitudes to needing to know an autonomous language in order to work in a respective community

	Cataluña	Valencia	I. Baleares	Galicia	P. Vasco	Navarra
Acuerdo	91	73	83	83	44	31
Desacuerdo	7	19	11	10	44	62
NS	2	6	6	6	12	6
NC	—	2	—	1	—	1
TOTAL	100	100	100	100	100	100
(N)	(1.007)	(771)	(473)	(681)	(615)	(452)

Source: Centro de Investigaciones Sociológicas 1994: 58

The attitudes towards the use of the local language shown in Table 10.2 would seem to suggest that at least the status planning in Catalonia and Galicia (if not the acquisition planning in the latter) is bearing fruit. This is far less clear in Euskadi.

■ How would you account for the less positive attitudes to the use of Basque, despite very active campaigning to promote its status?

■■ Whilst it is obviously important to have statistics on language use in order to guide the language-planning activities, what are the possible pitfalls in gathering these data, inherent in any questionnaires, interviewing, and so on? Think about how an interviewee might react if questioned in their mother tongue as opposed to in another, or what concepts like 'understand' or 'speak', mean in lay terms. Do you think a Castilian mother-tongue speaker might be more eager to support the promotion of the local language depending on which autonomous community they live in?

So far we have concentrated on the efforts to promote the languages in the linguistic minority communities. The evaluation of their success or failure has been judged partly in terms of statistical data from census and surveys. People's attitudes towards the languages themselves and their use is obviously also important, as we have seen in the last table and in the discussions in Chapter 5. We can see that there is a far greater feeling now in post-Franco Spain that the linguistic minorities have the right to use their languages, and, particularly in Catalonia, the pendulum of public opinion seems almost to have swung the other way. Recently, in fact, some disquiet about the role of Castilian in parts of Spain has begun to surface. In November 1994, the bastion of Castilian defence, the Real Academia Española (RAE), wrote a letter expressing these anxieties. These were reported in the Madrid-based national newspaper *El País*:

LA REAL ACADEMIA ESPAÑOLA PIDE MAS PROTECCION AL CASTELLANO EN LA COMUNIDADES BILINGÜES

Fernando Lázaro Carreter expresa su preocupación en una carta a Felipe González

En la carta se pone de relieve la preocupación 'ante los problemas de convivencia idomática, vivos hoy en las comunidades con lengua vernácula, así como por la creciente laxitud que se advierte en los usos públicos de la lengua española, tanto orales como escritos'.

Según la RAE [Real Academia Española] 'parece evidente que la personalidad de las comunidades autónomas con idioma territorial distinto del castellano se afianza legítimamente en el fomento y en el libre empleo de tales lenguas, felizmente reconocidos'. 'Pero no es menos cierto', continúa la carta, 'que la convivencia nacional tal como es regulada por el texto constitucional, exige garantizar las posibilidades de aprendizaje de la lengua común por parte de todos los españoles como medio espontáneo de expresión hablada o escrita, y su libre empleo, de tal modo que quede conjurada cualquier posibilidad de diglosia ... siendo necesario el bilingüismo para asegurar la convivencia pacífica de todas las lenguas de España.'

(El País 9.XI.94)

As a result of the RAE's anxieties about the '*laxitud*' in the use of Castilian, its director makes various hard-hitting suggestions to reverse this situation.

1 fomentar el bilingüismo real;
2 adoptar medidas que favorezcan 'una actitud no recelosa de todos los ciudadanos ante las distintas lenguas de España';
3 establecer planes de estudios para que la lengua española 'dote a todos los ciudadanos de destreza suficiente en su libre empleo, hablado y escrito';
4 hacer obligatorias ... 'las disciplinas escolares que afecten a España como nación';
5 'determinar las situaciones en que debe emplearse la lengua común para proteger a los ciudadanos como tales y en ejercicio de actividades que les crean obligaciones y derechos';
6 estipular la doble rotulación, en la lengua territorial y castellano, de todos los topónimos, incluidos los urbanos, con tradición en castellano;
7 disponer que las emisoras de radio y televisión dependientes del Estado emiten preferentemente en la lengua común.

(El País 9.XI.94)

■■ By stressing the need for a goal of bilingualism, the two sides in this debate appear to coincide. Do you think this is the case, or do you think the regional language planners might in fact now have grander designs, such as a predominance of (or even monolingualism in) the local language? Could this latter possibility become a reality?

■■   In number (4) what do you think is meant by *'disciplinas escolares que afecten España como nación'*? Remember the earlier discussion (in Chapter 1) about the relationship between education and national identity. For example, it is sometimes claimed that Catalan children only learn Catalan history nowadays.

■   In number (6) what are *'topónimos'*? Can you think of examples when the use of only one name might be a real linguistic problem? Outside Spain have you experienced other places where monolingual signage has been a challenge if you do not know the local language?

■■   Number (7) certainly flies in the face of the local language planning attempts to produce more and more media coverage in the local languages. Do you think there can be ways of compromising in this area? What are the drawbacks of using, for example, subtitling on television (see Chapter 7)?

Not surprisingly Basque and Catalan commentators were quick to denounce the Academy's letter as over-the-top and unnecessary, but it has certainly demonstrated an unease which now exists in some parts of Spain and amongst certain sections of the Spanish population towards the recent language-planning programmes. The mouthpiece of this disquiet has been, above all, the Madrid right-wing daily newspaper *ABC*. Perhaps its most notorious headline was when it compared Jordi Pujol, the President of the Catalan government, the Generalitat, to Franco, in an attempt to claim that Catalan language policies were now as oppressive to Castilian speakers as Franco's had been towards Catalan speakers.

IGUAL QUE FRANCO, PERO AL REVES: PERSECUCION DEL CASTELLANO EN CATALUÑA

El idioma catalán es uno de los grandes tesoros culturales de España ... Apoyar y ensalzar catalán en cambio de lo que hizo la dictadura es labor imprescindible de la Monarquía de todos, en beneficio de la cultura española. Pero reconocer lo que al catalán le corresponde, no supone que se tome a la vez una venganza provinciana y mezquina contra el castellano. Un hombre de tan buen sentido como Jordi Pujol debe ya tomar cartas en el asunto y evitar que desde ciertos organismos de la Generalidad, haciendo lo mismo que la Dictadura, algunos personajillos continúan con una campaña de persecución del castellano que alcanza en ocasiones límites grotescos. El castellano no sólo está definido en la Constitución como lengua a cuyo conocimiento tienen derecho todos los españoles, sino que se ha convertido en el segundo idioma del mundo, después del inglés.

(ABC 19.IX.93)

In the following chapter we will look in detail at how this is affecting the education system in Catalonia.

Current language planning in Latin America

In this chapter so far we have concentrated on seeing how recent language-planning activities have been taking place in post-Franco Spain. Language planning has of course also been taking place in Latin America. Here, too, constitutional frameworks have in some countries been changed, and in particular, updated to include a greater recognition for and protection of the non-Castilian, indigenous languages.

Language planning in contemporary Latin America focuses both on the planning (particularly at corpus level) of the dominant language, Spanish, and policies to improve the teaching and use of major indigenous languages. In a recent review of language planning in South America, Nancy Hornberger makes the point that we mention elsewhere (see Chapter 2 and Chapter 12) that there is considerable interest in the spread of Spanish at present, as a major world language, supported by the increasing population of Spanish speakers and such initiatives as the Instituto Cervantes (see Chapter 12). In a sense as a counter to this world-wide spread, some nations of Latin America are concerned to establish and protect their own identifiable variety of Spanish. The various Latin American language academies as well as cooperating with the RAE to defend Spanish in a universal sense, also serve as a base for exploring individual Latin American varieties.

■■ What do you see as being the problems or challenges that might exist for this sort of language policy? (Remind yourself of some of the points raised in Chapters 5 and 7.)

As Hornberger (1994: 222) suggests:

> . . . the question as to which Spanish language to promote is by no means easily resolved. Do Spanish Americans look to Spain for the definition of the prestige dialect of Spanish or is prestige defined in strictly Spanish American terms?

The answer to this question will obviously determine the kind of corpus planning to be pursued.

It is, however, in the area of the indigenous languages of Latin America where most planning activity and academic interest has taken place recently. There is little doubt that in modern Latin America Spanish is relentlessly making inroads into the language behaviour and use of indigenous communities.

■■ Discuss the reasons why this is likely to be happening. (Remember some of the issues raised in Chapter 2.)

The status planning of indigenous languages has constantly to contend with the high prestige and constant spread of Spanish in many Latin American countries. Their promotion and protection have also to over-come the problems of the deprived economic conditions in which the language planning must take place. The kind of resources available to, for example, the Catalan Generalitat can only be dreamt of by many Latin American language planners. As far as acquisition planning is concerned, we can find an encouraging activity in bilingual education provision in many parts of Latin America. This will be discussed more fully in the next chapter. One positive aspect of increased teaching of and in the indigenous languages is its spin-offs for corpus planning. If materials are to be produced and used, and learners encouraged to read, write and create through their native languages, then standard forms and codification of the languages become essential. This has been taking place in various parts, as Hornberger (1994) documents. She mentions indigenous language workshops which have been set up in Peru and in Mexico. She describes how these efforts have now extended to Ecuador, Peru and Bolivia, with the aims of preserving and elaborating these languages in written forms, and developing a written literary tradition (Hornberger 1994: 228).

Guatemala

Unfortunately in such limited space we cannot investigate the present language-planning activities of all the Latin American Spanish-speaking countries. However, we will look at the case of Guatemala as an example of a Latin American country which has recently changed its constitutional protection for its citizens' linguistic rights in recognition of the country's multiethnic and multilingual composition.

From the colonial period on, like so many other Latin American states, the language policies of Guatemala, such as there were, sought only to reinforce Castilian as the national language and to assimilate as quickly and cheaply as possible its large non-Castilian-speaking population to this dominant culture. More than 50 per cent of Guatemala's population are mother-tongue speakers of one of a range of Mayan languages (usually considered to be about twenty in all). Four of these languages have significant-sized populations. Many of the indigenous population are monolingual in their mother tongue only, posing very real issues for their involvement in Guatemalan society where Spanish only is the official language. In 1985 a new constitution was passed which signalled an important shift in this policy with the recognition of the indigenous peoples' rights. Various articles of this constitution underpin an improvement in the status of Guatemala's indigenous communities, as outlined by Richards (1989):

Article 58

[The Constitution recognises] the rights of peoples and communities to their cultural identity, in accord with their values, their language and their customs . . .

Article 66

The State recognises, respects and promotes [the Mayan] forms of life, customs, traditions, forms of social organization, the use of indigenous dress by men and women, languages and dialects.

Article 76

. . . In the schools established in the predominantly Indian zones that instruction should preferably be imparted in bilingual form.

Article 143

[The Mayan languages form part of] the cultural patrimony of the nation.

(all cited in Richards 1989: 93)

Besides improving the status of the Mayan languages, this new constitution helped to encourage acquisition planning through the setting up of bilingual and bicultural education programmes in the eighties. To do this there was a need to standardise and elaborate spelling and vocabulary norms for the Mayan languages. Richards (1989: 104–113) describes in detail these corpus-planning moves.

Education is probably the key area to promote the indigenous languages in Guatemala, as is so often the case in Latin America, a point which we will develop further in the next chapter. However, the improved prestige for the Mayan languages has encouraged their wider use by more people, and, importantly, in a far wider range of functions in the public domain. As we see elsewhere (Chapters 7, 8 and 11) the use of the media, in the form of radio broadcasts, also helped to promote the languages.

■■■ Choose another Latin American country with a significant non-Castilian-speaking population and see what language-planning activities they are pursuing. Examine the constitutional and legal framework, the diversity of the languages spoken, the existence of any written norms, the degree of use of the languages in urban areas, the education programmes and the extent of use of the languages in the media (see, for example, Hamel 1994a and 1994b).

Further reading

For good introductions to the concepts of language planning, see Fasold (1994); Wardaugh (1992) and Cooper (1989). For a good introductory overview of the state of the minority languages in post-Franco Spain, see Siguan (1992). For current language planning in South America, see Hornberger (1994). For detailed discussion of Latin American constitutions and language rights, see Alvar López (1986, Chapter 10).

•　　•　　•

Chapter 11

Language
and education

Chapter 11

E DUCATION is arguably the single most important aspect of language planning. Through education policies corpus planning can be reinforced as children are taught the prescribed form of a language; status planning can be enhanced when the importance of a particular language is emphasised by its role in the curriculum; and of course acquisition planning is centrally realised through education programmes, both for children and adults.

In this chapter we will first look at the possible different types of language programmes in education systems in general, and then take Latin American and Spanish cases to exemplify these categories. It will be seen how controversial and emotional the choices of language education programmes currently are in parts of the Spanish-speaking world, clearly underlying the role they play in the protection and status of their speakers' communities.

Language becomes an issue for education and language planning not only in terms of which languages are taught, but, above all, in terms of the language through which education is given. What is the language of the classroom, the text books and the playground? Language programmes vary from simply teaching a language as a foreign language – one more subject on the timetable – through various types of bilingual programmes, to total immersion in a language different from that spoken at home or in the immediate environment. An important issue regarding the language of education is of course the use of the mother tongue.

■ In 1951 UNESCO declared its support for the desirability of every child at least starting their education in their mother tongue. What are the obvious practical problems of this directive? Consider how you define a 'mother tongue' in an entirely multilingual society. Who trains the teachers? Who produces the books and materials? What happens when a school serves a very wide-ranging multilingual community?

■ In 1968 a Bilingual Education Act was passed in the USA. As a result, in some states where there were high levels of non-English-speaking immigrant children, many of whom were Spanish-speaking, attempts were made to teach them through their mother tongue for a period, until it was felt they could integrate into mainstream English-medium education. Why does this mother-tongue teaching stop after a limited period?

- In 1977 the European Community issued a directive encouraging member states to provide mother-tongue language programmes for the children of immigrants within these states. In those states which complied with the directive, this often took the form of classes held either after school or at the weekends. Why might this send negative messages to these learners? Are you aware of schools in Britain where mother-tongue teaching takes place?

Bilingual education programmes

To discover which programme is most likely to suit language-planning purposes we need to examine the objectives of the different language education programmes. It is usual to divide the objectives of **bilingual education** into two broad categories: the **assimilationist** (or **transitional**) and the **maintenance** (or **pluralist**) models.

- As with the American example mentioned above, by far the most common model of bilingual education is the assimilationist model. Why might language planners favour this model?

- In the maintenance model of bilingual education the two languages are used side by side throughout the child's schooling, being granted equal status and equal time. Can you think of examples of where this system operates? Can you see difficulties in making this actually work? For example, is the status of a science class perceived as equal to that of an art class? How could this sort of problem (if it is one) be countered? How could we get over the problem that more text books are available in certain languages (which?) than others?

Frequently, bilingual education does not start straight away, the child begins learning in its mother tongue and gradually the second language is introduced – in many cases eventually to replace the mother tongue altogether.

Monolingual language education is also used at primary level in two other types of programme: submersion and immersion programmes. The former, rather than being any pedagogically informed method, is simply a name for the inevitable linguistic change which is forced on many children the world over once they start school and have to learn the language of their state (which is not their mother tongue). Many non-Castilian mother-tongue speakers undergo this experience when entering school in Latin America. During the Franco period all of Spain's linguistic minority children had to face this prospect, if they had not already started to learn Castilian at home. On the other hand, the latter, the immersion method, is used – voluntarily – as a way of teaching children the majority language of their immediate community, often where that language is in fact a minority language at a national level. Examples of this include French to English speakers in Quebec, or Catalan to Castilian speakers in Catalonia. The extent to which this immersion approach remains truly voluntary is politically and socially very important, as we shall see.

Language education and literacy in Latin America

Access to education and the role of literacy in society are further crucial issues to be discussed when thinking about language education. This is particularly true in developing countries where typically much of the population has not had the opportunity to receive much if any education, and therefore has had limited opportunities to acquire languages, and above all literacy skills. The role of literacy in language planning is therefore also very interesting. In twentieth-century Latin America it has been a very important and sensitive issue.

Up until well into this century the provision of education in Latin American countries has been poor and restricted to the middle and upper classes.

■ To some extent the under-education of the workforce was a deliberate policy by the landowning elites. Why do you think that this was the case? What might have been the disadvantages to the landowners if their workers were better educated?

Even as provision improved, however, it often reflected the state's desire to shape the indigenous people into Europeanised culture and ways of being. Originally the indigenous populations learnt Spanish, not through any formal education system, but through contact with Spanish speakers and the inevitable need to communicate and transact with them. Even as more education became available, however, its principal purpose was to assimilate all the population into the Europeanised value systems.

■■ Consider some of the ways in which the culture and values of the Spanish-speaking elites were presented in contrast with those of the indigenous Latin Americans. The contrast between backward/ primitive and modern/civilised is a common theme in tensions between majority and minority groups. Even the way the majority and minority communities refer to each other can carry hidden values. What are some of these names?

As we have noted already (see Chapter 2), literacy plays an important part in the construction of national identity in the relatively new states of Latin America, as issues of citizenship and legal rights are bound up with it. The modernisation of the late twentieth century has made this form of access to power even more important. Literacy programmes can help previously disenfranchised groups both to become more integrated into the political processes of their society, and to be made more aware of their own identities. This may actually challenge some of their own values, such as attitudes to the role of women. The experience of literacy campaigns in such places as Nicaragua, Chile and Bolivia has certainly demonstrated this. Recent literacy programmes have been ambiguous about issues of language. Some, like the highly acclaimed Nicaraguan Sandinista literacy programme, originally failed to see the important link between literacy–language–identity, and sought to teach literacy through Spanish only to groups for whom Spanish was not their mother tongue. The Nicaraguans, fortunately, rectified this in a short space of time.

■ In what ways might the consequence of this type of mistake be very serious? The very policy of empowerment through literacy can make people more aware of their cultural differences and as a result, realise the lack of recognition of these from the central government.

In places such as Ecuador and Bolivia, literacy has been promoted through indigenous languages, but this in turn can raise other difficult questions, such as the fact that Westernised literacy concepts are based, of course, on a written tradition.

- Does this make sense for languages with entirely oral traditions? Will these peoples ever have the need to read or write in their non-Spanish languages? What kind of written materials would encourage them to want to read and write in their native languages?

- With the huge levels of migration of indigenous peoples to the cities, will they use their native languages for urban, Western ways? Keeping in contact with their families in rural areas has led to the need to write letters (and to have them read). Is this a possible motive for increasing literacy in indigenous languages, or does one assume that eventually modern technology in the form of telephones will make this unnecessary before it has really happened?

- Is some form of literacy (even radioliteracy, see Chapters 7 and 8), indeed, the only way of preserving the existence of endangered lesser used languages in modern society? (For an interesting and polemic negative answer to this question, see Mühlhäusler 1990.)

As the division between urban and rural life becomes more blurred, with the inevitable expansion of modern technological forms of communications and transportation, such media as radio and television (even computers) will increasingly challenge reading/writing literacies. It may well be that the oral traditions of much of Latin America's indigenous population are more suited to these forms of literacy than the traditional forms of reading and writing. The literacy programmes, however, have shown that the indigenous population wants to learn through Spanish, the language they perceive as the vehicle of social mobility and access to power structures. In this sense the issue of which language to learn and the issues of the appropriateness of literacy to indigenous cultures come together.

Lastra (1992) refers to an extensive survey on education in Latin America carried out by Utta von Gleich (1989) in which the latter is fairly pessimistic about the extent to which bilingual education in Latin America is much more than transitional to Castilianisation even today, believing that it is far from the bilingual/bicultural model that some are claiming for it.

El objetivo sociopolítico de la educación bilingüe en Hispanoamérica es, según Gleich, la inserción de los grupos marginales en la sociedad nacional. Se le llama a este objetivo integración, por oposición a asimilación, que se usa en sentido negativo ... [E]n casi todas las constituciones se declara al español como lengua oficial. A las lenguas indígenas se les concede el estatus de lenguas nacionales o bien son admitidas como lenguas de instrucción a nivel de la primaria ... [H]ay mucha diferencia entre emplear las lenguas en el ámbito de la educación primaria y el tipo de autonomía de los vascos o los catalanes ...

Al revisar las constituciones y las leyes sobre educación de los países de habla española se ve claramente que ninguna de las lenguas indígenas tiene el mismo estatus que el español.

(Lastra 1992: 466)

The two case studies below will show that, indeed, the Spanish situation is more favourable to the teaching of the minority language, Catalan, than, for example, the Bolivian context is for its indigenous languages, but that even in Catalonia the provision of bilingual education programmes is not unproblematic.

■■ When you have read the two case studies, and including any other information you have on bilingual education in Spanish-speaking countries, discuss the reality of programmes whose declared aim is to make two languages, one the language of the state and the other a minoritised language, truly equal. Suggest where this may be genuinely successful, and where it manifestly is not.

Case study 1: Bolivia

■■■ From whatever sources you have available to you – books, journals, videos, databases, and native Bolivians – find out as much as you can about contemporary Bolivia. Create for yourself a picture of its linguistic configuration. You will need to understand its history, its geography, the size of its population, its different ethnic groups, what languages they speak, the distribution of rural to urban population concentrations, its economy and social conditions. This information will give you the necessary background to understand and assess the current developments and issues of Bolivia's education policies as regards language learning.

Bolivia is, like many Latin American countries, a multicultural and multilingual country. There are high proportions of speakers of Aymara (approximately 23 per cent of the total population) and Quechua (approximately 35 per cent), as well as speakers of at least another thirty indigenous languages, some of which comprise very small speech communities (Chiodi 1990). Alongside these, of course, Spanish dominates as the language of power and urban elites, although, notably, as late as 1976 census figures show that monolingualism in Spanish is found in a minority of the Bolivian population, i.e. 37 per cent (Chiodi 1990).

The existence of both Andean and tropical jungle regions ensures diversity and impedes easy access, keeping small, indigenous communities relatively marginalised from modern society. These groups have also through the centuries suffered exploitation from landowners and, particularly, mine owners, leading to appalling conditions and early death. The result of economic hardship, as in other Andean nations, has often been forced migration to the cities. This has created large sprawling shanty-town settlements around cities such as La Paz, where conditions are harsh and the residents are barely integrated into modern urban life. Many of these new city dwellers speak little Spanish, particularly the women. They are, however, eager to learn Spanish and to have their children educated in Spanish as they perceive it as the language required for social advancement.

Despite this diverse multilingual picture, Plaza and Albó (1989: 70) describe the Bolivian education system thus:

> En resumen, pese a las características pluriculturales de la realidad Boliviana, hasta el día de hoy la práctica casi universal es que en todo el sistema escolar, desde pre-básico hasta la universidad, se impone el castellano, y en el campo incluso se castiga el uso de lengua vernácula.

- Stories (often actual memories) of punishment for the use of a home language not accepted at school abound the world over. Do you know of examples of this in language communities you are familiar with or have studied?

- Plaza and Albó talk about how education in Bolivia not only tends to 'Castilianise' children, but also offers a curriculum which is basically 'occidentalizante' and 'modernizante'. Discuss what you think they mean by these two adjectives.

Alongside this majority trend towards an education system which sought to 'Castilianise' the indigenous children, some small but significant steps were taken, mostly in the 1970s and 1980s, to introduce bilingual education programmes, as Plaza and Albó document (1989: 72–77). These attempts range from a strictly transitional model of bilingual education (in particular that practised by the Summer Institute of Linguistics) to more 'maintenance'-type models for either Aymara-Castilian or Quechua-Castilian.

- ■ The Summer Institute of Linguistics has had an important, and sometimes controversial, role to play in education and language teaching in Latin America. Try to find out more about this organisation and its aims and objectives. Where else has it had a significant impact? Consider in general the role of missionaries in the education of indigenous populations in Latin America in the twentieth century. (See, for example, Barros 1995.)

The problems encountered in these various bilingual programmes which Plaza and Albó list are familiar ones to language planners in regions attempting to promote indigenous languages and minoritised languages: poor resources, under-trained and few teachers, the lack of materials, unfavourable attitudes, both from those who might back the programmes and those who receive them. As Plaza and Albó comment (1989: 76):

> La educación bilingüe sólo puede ser implementada si recibe el apoyo de las autoridades respectivas y se generen las condiciones materiales (salarios, textos, metodologías, etc.). Pero todo esto no será posible si además – condición sine que non – no se produce un cambio substancial en las actitudes lingüísticas, que a pesar de los avances, en la actualidad continúan favoreciendo el castellano y despreciando a las lenguas nativas.

In more recent years a combination of private funding (usually from non-government organisations, NGOs) and some state support has resulted in some exciting new projects in bilingual education being developed in Bolivia. In particular, very recent state-sponsored bilingual education programmes of a genuinely intercultural nature have been launched, modelled largely on Peruvian schemes; it is too early yet to assess their success. These, however, are primarily in the area of non-formal education, aimed above all at adults, and often women in particular. As we have already noted in previous chapters (see Chapter 7 and Chapter 8) literacy programmes have been focusing on the very specific needs of these indigenous communities, especially when they have had to migrate to an unfamiliar, westernised urban situation. The programmes have challenged the traditional view of literacy as entirely writing-based, and developed the use of radio as a way of teaching and consolidating the use of indigenous languages. Spanish is still being taught, and is clearly wanted and needed by the indigenous groups, but it is being presented in parallel with Aymara and Quechua for these adults, rather than instead of their mother tongues.

■■   Do you think that a change in attitudes and perceptions towards the indigenous languages and Castilian by these adults will have an impact on what they want for the education of their children? Can you see this leading to any changes in the school-level education system?

Case study 2: Catalonia

Language education has been and continues to be a highly emotive topic in Catalonia since the creation of the Autonomous Community and the legalising and promotion of the teaching of Catalan. Initially, Catalan was introduced into the school system without much opposition and with enthusiastic support from many to whom the study of their mother tongue had been denied throughout the Franco years. The results have been impressive in terms of knowledge and favourable attitudes to Catalan.

Although a predominantly urban society without the general education problems of many parts of Latin America, Catalonia also had to face the challenge of providing non-formal language learning for adults. This took the form both of the teaching of literacy (in the strictly traditional sense) to Catalans who spoke the language but had not been allowed to learn it at school, as well as a full programme of communicative language teaching to those non-Catalan speakers now settled in Catalonia, many of whom had only a very basic education and grasp of literacy skills.

■   What are the potential dangers of teaching native speakers and non-native speakers in the same language programme? This is a common problem found in many parts where provision in minority languages is restricted and therefore mother-tongue learners and second-language learners have to study together.

Articles 14–20 of the Catalan Linguistic Normalisation Law of 1983 set out the position of Catalan in the education system. It is worth quoting Article 14 in full as it is the section which establishes the main principles and has been under review for its constitutionality:

Artículo 14

1   El catalán como lengua propia de Cataluña, lo es también de la enseñanza en todos los niveles educativos.
2   Los niños tienen derecho a recibir la primera enseñanza en su lengua habitual, ya sea ésta el catalán o el castellano. La Administración debe garantizar este derecho y poner los medios necesarios para hacerlo efectivo. Los padres o los tutores pueden ejercerlo en nombre de sus hijos instando a que se aplique.
3   La lengua catalana y la lengua castellana deben ser enseñadas obligatoriamente en todos los niveles y los grados de la enseñanza no universitaria.
4   Todos los niños de Cataluña, cualquiera que sea su lengua habitual al iniciar la enseñanza, deben poder utilizar normal y correctamente el catalán y el castellano al final de sus estudios básicos.
5   La Administración debe tomar las medidas convenientes para que (a) los alumnos no sean separados en centros distintos por razones de lengua; (b) la lengua catalana sea utilizada progresivamente a medida que todos los alumnos la vayan dominando.

And Article 20 states that:

> Los Centros de enseñanza han de hacer de la lengua catalana vehículo de expresión normal, tanto en las actividades internas, como en las de proyección externa.

Implicitly or explicitly the overwhelming message from this section of the Law is the intention to use the education system as a central part of the promotion and expansion of Catalan.

The implementation of the Law, and specifically the part concerning the education system, has been steady and with notable success. In the case of the education system, the initial result was a discreet but important introduction of more Catalan in the schools and the beginning of the so-called Immersion method, modelled to a large extent on the Canadian programme.

An important change, however, took place in the education system as the result of the Spanish state introducing centrally a major educational reform – the *Ley Orgánica de Ordenación General del Sistema Educativo* (LOGSE) – which was used as an opportunity for the Catalan Government to accelerate the amount of Catalan used in schools. In particular the immersion programme which had been a voluntary programme requiring approval by a school's '*consejo*' (i.e. governing body) was decreed in March 1992 by the Catalan Government to be an essential part of their education programme.

The immersion method is used in schools in predominantly Castilian-speaking areas where the child is immersed in Catalan the moment he or she begins schooling (often as young as three years old). The medium of instruction and of general communication within the school is Catalan. In many of these schools no Castilian at all is introduced until as late as seven or eight years of age. In the early days of the immersion programme these schools proved popular with many Castilian-speaking parents who, often working-class immigrants from the poorer south, saw this as an essential part of their children's chances of social improvement and mobility. Such are the attitudes to the prestige of Catalan and its role in Catalan society that most felt it important that their children should learn Catalan as early as possible. From the 1993–94 school year these programmes became compulsory rather than voluntary, and with this change emerged various signs of protest and dissent.

An important premise of the new LOGSE is to require that the formulation of goals and curricular content should be decided by the individual schools, in accordance with certain basic overall principles set out in the new reform law. The justification for this apparent flexibility in delegating the exact shape and structure to the individual schools is explained in an article in *El País*:

> Una [modificación] es la obligatoriedad de elaborar un diseño curricular propio del centro ajustado a las necesidades del alumnado y del entorno.
>
> (*El País* 18.IX.93)

In the case of Catalonia the Generalitat has interpreted this as necessitating certain particular linguistic goals in order to meet the needs of the pupils and their environment. Indeed the Generalitat took the statement of intent in the Linguistic Normalisation Law as the basis for this interpretation. In a decree published in March 1992 it stated that:

El Catalán como lengua propia de Cataluña lo es también de la enseñanza. *Se utilizará normalmente como lengua vehicular y de aprendizaje* de la educación infantil, de la educación primaria y de la educación secundaria obligatoria.

(author's italics)

The link between '*lengua propia*' and '*lengua vehicular y de aprendizaje*' with '*las necesidades del alumnado y del entorno*' has created the justification for a far more aggressive insistence on the integration of Castilian-speaking children into Catalan school environments. This has certainly incited strong reactions from some quarters, although not always from within Catalonia itself.

Another important aspect of the Linguistic Normalisation Law is enshrined in Article 14.5 which insists on the undesirability of separating children into different schools according to their languages. This remains a firm conviction of the Generalitat who argue that to do so would be to run the risk of marginalising those children with Castilian as their mother tongue. This has also become a point of contention in the present debate.

It was, above all, the change, in the 1993–94 school year, to implement the immersion programmes throughout Catalonia which has provided the spark that ignited vociferous (although small in numbers) opposition to the teaching of Catalan, or, more particularly, to the absence of any Castilian until, in many cases, the age of seven. Organisations such as CADECA (Coordinadora de Afectados por la Defensa de la Lengua Castellana), or la Asociación por la Tolerancia y contra la Discriminación, or Acción Cultural Miguel de Cervantes, amongst others, have sprung up. These groups, led by the right-wing lawyer Esteban Gómez Rovira, have put their arguments through the press and through the courts. They appear to be a very small minority: by May 1994 fewer than fifty families had brought complaints or individual cases. The spokesperson for the Asociación por la Tolerancia, Antonio Robles, insists that there is much covert support, but that people are frightened to make their opinions public (*ABC* 13.VIII.94).

■■ Can you think of reasons why this reticence to come into the open might exist? Compare this with attitudes to teaching Catalan during the Franco years.

A survey commissioned by the Catalan daily *Avui* and carried out in February 1994 by the Institut EMB Yankelovich found that 98 per cent of the parents interviewed wanted their children to learn Catalan in school, and 86 per cent rejected the idea of different schools for different languages (*Avui* 6.II.94). In another survey carried out by the Spanish Centro de Investigaciones Sociológicas in May 1994, it emerged that only 4 per cent of residents in Catalonia do not understand Catalan (*The Times* 27.V.94). In this same survey 96 per cent believed that everyone residing in Catalonia should understand Catalan, and 82 per cent believed that public sector employees should be fluent in Catalan. Whilst clearly there is significant opposition from an articulate minority in Catalonia about the present language education policies, it would appear that the majority are still happy with the situation.

Conclusion

We can see from these two case studies just how closely language education policies reflect the social priorities, attitudes and political motives of the communities where they are being implemented. As is the case in general and not just for matters relating to languages, education is a microcosm of society and both reacts to its concerns and proacts in order to influence society. Many of the other places given as examples of particular language issues throughout the book – Mexico, Puerto Rico, the Basque Country, Paraguay – are directly affected in these issues by what is happening in their schools and education systems, both state-run and privately-organised.

Further reading

Various names stand out in the very wide literature on bilingual education, the work by Skutnabb-Kangas (1981) is probably amongst the most important. On bilingualism in Latin America, see von Gleich (1989), Hornberger (1992; 1994) and Chiodi (1990), which is also particularly useful on Bolivia. For discussion of bilingual education in Spain, see Siguan (1980; 1982). The Catalan Generalitat, the Basque Government, and the Galician Xunta all publish pamphlets and books on their education laws, the impact of these on the curriculum, and re-training programmes for teachers.

• • •

The vitality
of Spanish today

Chapter 12

T HROUGHOUT THE BOOK we have observed how Spanish has spread, particularly through its colonial designs across Latin America. This spread continues; the extent and nature of its continuing expansion will be the subject of this concluding chapter.

So far we have concentrated on Spain and, to a lesser extent, Latin America. Here we will focus on the significant Spanish-speaking population of the USA, as well as the rather particular case of Puerto Rico. Some of the lessons we can draw from these two areas will also help in pulling together conclusions about general trends and implications for the future of the Spanish language.

Spanish speakers in the USA

The population data on USA residents of Spanish-speaking origin is particularly unreliable, reflecting as it does the unsettled nature of parts of this population (migrant workers doing seasonal work), and, more importantly, the fact that a sizeable proportion of these people have entered the USA illegally. This community is concentrated principally in nine states, in seven of which (New Mexico, California, Texas, Arizona, New York, Florida and Colorado) Hispanics account for more than 10 per cent of the state's population.

Estimates of the numbers of residents of Spanish-speaking origin in the USA by the 1990s vary widely. The official figures of the 1993 Current Population Survey (CPS) report 22.8 million, which represents 8.9 per cent of the total US population. What is certain is that this is an expanding population. One of the factors which contribute to this continuing expansion is shared by all Latin American populations, the high birth rate. Moreover, immigration from Latin American countries to the USA is still continuing, as relatives join settled family members in search of better economic conditions.

■■ The 'Hispanics' of the USA in fact form the fourth largest Spanish-speaking population in the world. This significant population is nonetheless a *minority* within the state where it resides. It is also an underprivileged, marginalised minority. Discuss the paradox of this situation.

Whatever the exact numbers, it is certainly a significant population, which, along with the fact that much of it is intensely concentrated in relatively few regions, contributes to a sense, sometimes even fear, by other Americans that there is a creeping Hispanic takeover of US society. Whilst this is clearly an exaggeration, the feelings nonetheless persist and have led to strong reactions against this community, and are sometimes expressed through linguistic discrimination. This opposition has been particularly vociferous through the 'English Only' campaigns, which seek to identify a sense of American-ness by claiming the English language as one of its incontrovertible characteristics (see Fishman 1989). The American Constitution does not specifically designate any language as the national language, and, although in the past all immigrants arriving in the USA have immediately set about learning English, it has always been implicitly understood that the Constitution protects the right to retain one's mother tongue. The 'English Only' campaign has not been able to go so far as to change the national constitution, but has succeeded in bringing about the passing of various amendments at state level, notably in California in November 1986. Here an amendment to the State Constitution making English the only official language was passed by an overwhelming majority of 73.2 per cent of the Californian electorate, in a state where Hispanics constitute more than 20 per cent of the population.

Although this group is frequently referred to as the *Hispanic* community, as we can see from Table 12.1 this word ignores the diversity of the group. These immigrants come from various different countries of origin, principally Mexico, Puerto Rico and Cuba.

To lump all Hispanics together is as wrong as considering all Latin Americans are the same. They bring with them to the USA diverse cultural, social and political backgrounds, and they also have significant linguistic differences. However, preferring to call themselves *Latinos*, over recent years, members of this diverse group, and particularly those born in the USA, have begun to see the advantage of working together to support and defend their rights.

Various linguistic issues are of interest when considering this community. Obviously of greatest significance to us is to predict the extent to which Spanish will survive as the mother tongue, or, at least, one of two bilingual partner languages for the members of this group. Unlike many

TABLE 12.1 Persons of Hispanic origin, March 1993

	Millions	Percentage of total Hispanic population
Total	22.8	100
Mexican	14.6	64.3
Puerto Rican	2.4	10.6
Cuban	1.1	4.7
Central/S. America	3.1	13.4
Other Hispanics	1.6	7.0

Source: Current Population Survey (CPS) 1993

immigrant groups to settle in the USA over the centuries, the Spanish-speaking community has kept its language alive, and even contains sizeable groups of monolingual Spanish speakers. The reasons for this probably lie with the fact that their countries of origin are closer than those of other immigrant groups.

■ In what way would this make Spanish easier to retain? Consider geographical factors, but also technological factors of the twentieth century, such as TV and telephones.

Nonetheless, a shift away from Spanish and to greater, or total, use of English is observed in second-generation Hispanics. This is, however, a complex picture involving differences of generation, age and economic characteristics. It does seem that Spanish is not only spoken more by the older generation, but that the younger generation tends to use Spanish largely only with older members of the community.

■■ If inter-generational language transmission appears not to take place, can a language survive? Do other factors contribute to keeping its use alive? Why might this Spanish example be different from a lesser-spoken language like Basque?

The maintenance of Spanish use is obviously greater in areas where these speakers are highly concentrated, particularly in Miami, New York, Texas and California, where new immigration, too, reinforces its use. These are areas also, however, where bilingual education programmes have been introduced, which, as we have already seen, usually aim to integrate and assimilate the Spanish-speaking child into mainstream US education as an English speaker, who is encouraged to discard his or her linguistic heritage.

Although there are very few educational projects in the USA to help teach and maintain the use of mother-tongue Spanish, and particularly literacy in Spanish, there do exist a certain number of newspapers written in Spanish, and Spanish is used in some areas as a vehicle of written communication. However, insofar as many 'Hispanics' are members of very under-privileged and marginalised groups, their need or desire for literacy, in any language, is restricted. Cultural links, if not always linguistic ones, also help to retain a sense of Hispanic culture, with the celebration of religious and folk *fiestas*, family reunions and certain eating and drinking norms, often provided for by Hispanic-run shops.

Nonetheless two predictable and noteworthy phenomena can be seen to be emerging in the US Spanish-speaking community: **codeswitching** and linguistic 'homogenisation'. Many observers have analysed the high level of codeswitching between Spanish and English which takes place within this community. This may be at the sentence level or even word level. It may also include the anglicising of Spanish words and syntax, for example, translating phrasal verbs or using an English word with a Spanish shape (see Zentella 1990 for examples). This code-switching is so complex that it follows its own internal rules which are shared and understood by its users, creating a separate linguistic variety.

■ Could this variety be said to be a separate dialect or language? Does it fulfil the criteria you identified in Chapter 1 for a dialect or language to exist? Or is this just a transitional phase on the way to total monolingualism in English? (For further information on code-switching, see Appel and Muysken 1987, Chapter 10.)

One of the leading commentators on the Spanish-speaking community in the USA and herself a member of this community is Ana Celia Zentella. In her article investigating the linguistic worlds of Puerto Ricans who find themselves belonging to (but on the margins of) both US Hispanic society and Puerto Rican society, she quotes from a poem by the American-Puerto Rican writer Henry L. Padron as an example of both the phenomenon of codeswitching and the frustrations it brings in terms of self identity and expression. Its title 'Dos Worlds – Two Mundos' sums up this dilemma.

As well as this variety created by codeswitching, another pan-US Hispanic dialect is emerging, as those features particular to, for example, Mexican or Cuban Spanish are being replaced with a more general Spanish, which we might call the Spanish of the USA. This is particularly the case with the Spanish-language TV programming which is available in many parts of the USA. (See also Chapter 7 for a discussion of the homogenisation of language through the media.)

Puerto Rico and the language question

Because of Puerto Rico's ambiguous relation with the USA – that of an unincorporated territory – language, as is so often the case, has been symbolic of the island's identity struggles. The early domination of Puerto Rico by the USA was reflected in the 1902 law making English and Spanish the official languages. In recent years language has been the emblem of the debate over closer ties with the USA versus independence. Those proposing Spanish as the sole official language have normally been fearful of Puerto Rico becoming a fully fledged American state, and many wished for total independence from the USA. These overtly political motives for making Spanish the sole official language are given support by the fact that the majority of the island's population (about 80 per cent) is monolingual Spanish-speaking, and whilst the rest are bilingual Spanish-English, many have only limited English.

■■ There is a strange irony here that the 'colonial' language being 'imposed' is English whilst apparently the 'natural' language is Spanish. However, of course Spanish was in fact the colonial language brought to the island by the Spanish conquerors, and is no more native to Puerto Rico than English. What does this tell us about a possible global hierarchy of languages? Does the negative impact of linguistic colonisation inevitably lead communities to look for another linguistic variety to nail their identity to, wherever that variety in fact originated from?

In April 1991 this campaign to make Spanish the only official language resulted in a new language law being passed declaring just that. As we shall see later, it was heralded not only as a victory for Puerto Rican nationalism, but also for supporters of Spanish generally, and aroused much interest back in Spain. But this victory was short-lived; in 1993 the party wishing for closer ties with the USA won the elections and immediately re-introduced the co-official status of Spanish and English.

In terms of the role of Spanish as a world language the reaction to the 1991 language law amongst the world's Spanish-speaking community is relevant. A particularly strident article in the Spanish daily *El Independiente* sums this up:

EL ESPAÑOL LIBRA MAÑANA SU BATALLA DECISIVA CON EL INGLES EN PUERTO RICO

La Cámara de Representantes decretará el castellano único idioma oficial de la isla.

> La Cámara de representantes de Puerto Rico decretará mañana el castellano como único idioma oficial de la isla, honor que, hasta el momento, compartía con el inglés, al ser un Estado asociado de los Estados Unidos. Este triunfo del idioma de Cervantes sobre el de Shakespeare no hace sino corroborar el buen momento que atraviesa el español al nivel internacional, al unirse a la obtención de los dos últimos premios Nobel de Literatura por escritores hispanos y a la reciente creación del Instituto Cervantes.
>
> (*El Independiente* 4.IV.91)

- Notice the irony of the reference here to the 'Greats' of the two respective languages in both cases being Europeans, i.e. Cervantes and Shakespeare. Does this not seem a strange reference, given that the Spanish of Puerto Rico obviously has more in common with other Latin American varieties, and the English of the island is manifestly that of the USA? This eurocentric view contrasts particularly with the fact that the two Nobel Prize winners referred to here were in fact Latin Americans!

One could argue that this is a pretty chauvinistic piece of journalism on the part of the Madrid-based daily. The Puerto Rican language law is seen as one more feather in the cap of the Spanish language as a vehicle of international communication. This triumphal tone is also seen in an article two days later in another Madrid newspaper *ABC* headlined '*El español gana la batalla al inglés en Puerto Rico*'. It goes on to describe the ceremony of the signing of the new law

> En el ambiente del salón de actos del Centro [de Bellas Artes] se respiraba ese espíritu, en lo que fue una verdadera fiesta de declaración hispana en torno al idioma . . .

The closing speech of this ceremony was given by Manuel Alvar, the then director of the Spanish Royal Academy. Once again the role of the RAE in underlining the importance of Castilian is highlighted by his participation.

In this moment of euphoria for the victory of the Spanish language over English (a victory admittedly that would be turned around two years later) the Barcelona-based daily *La Vanguardia* draws an interesting parallel between the situation of Puerto Rico and that of Catalonia, noting the symbolism of language in both cases.

> En cierta manera podríamos establecer un paralelismo entre Puerto Rico y aquellas autonomías como Cataluña y el País Vasco que también, en el marco de la Constitución española, gozan de una condición especial. De acuerdo con el prólogo de la Constitución puertorriqueña de 1952, son valores especiales 'factores determinantes en nuestra vida la ciudadanía de los EEUU de América' y 'la lealtad a los postulados de la Constitución federal' así como 'la convivencia en Puerto Rico de las dos grandes culturas del hemisferio americano'.

The article's Catalan author, Josep Miró i Ardevol, takes this parallel to a highly controversial conclusion:

> Será bueno que la misma unanimidad y congratulaciones que la cultura y política españolas han generado al saludar la decisión de Puerto Rico acogieran ahora en esta otra propuesta una lengua hermana, el catalán, para así facilitar lo que, más pronto o más tarde, será una realidad, que la lengua propia de los catalanes sea la única oficial de esta nación.
>
> (*La Vanguardia* 22.V.91)

■ Do you find this comparison of the two situations convincing? Do you think that there is the same danger of not protecting English speakers' rights in Puerto Rico as is perceived to be a threat for Castilian speakers in Catalonia?

It is interesting that just as the Catalans feel they are oppressed and dominated by the majority Castilian speakers, those who oppose moves to closer ties with the USA express their anxieties in similar ways, not least through the importance they accord Spanish. One of the chief proponents of Spanish as sole official language, and the Governor who signed the 1991 law, is Rafael Hernández Colón. Shortly after the defeat of his party in the November 1992 elections he wrote in support of Puerto Rico's separate identity from that of the USA:

> Somos pueblos, nacionalidades diferentes con un vínculo común que es la ciudadanía, pero que en la realidad de la lengua, las tradiciones, las costumbres, la visión de la vida misma, no somos homogéneos . . . Nuestra cultura es una fuerza irreductible, es y será una realidad operante que no se ajusta a la homogeneidad que requiere el convertirse en un Estado más de Estados Unidos.
>
> (*ABC* 17.XI.92)

■■ In what way could the pressure to 'homogenise' cultures and languages in attempts to bring communities together across larger and larger areas effect the future of Spanish?

Spanish in the late twentieth century

As we have seen, the role of Spanish as identity marker continues to be an important factor in areas where its use is still very much under discussion, whether this be among the large Spanish-speaking group in the USA, or with continuing defence of its status in Puerto Rico or in post-Franco Spain. On the one hand its position is affected by the minority languages spoken around it (or, majority, in the case of the Hispanics in the USA), on the other, the most important influence in the late twentieth century on linguistic behaviour is the expanding use of English.

■■ How do you think Spanish might be affected by these two pincer movements on its growth and development?

In an article in *El País* in May 1995 the respected Spanish writer Francisco Ayala discussed the '*Vitalidad actual de la lengua española*'. He compares its present health to that of other major languages:

> En los momentos actuales la lengua española, como en verdad todas las lenguas del mundo, empezando por la invasora inglesa, atraviesa una fase de rápida transformación, a resulta de los cambios acarreados por el fabuloso progreso tecnológico de los ultimos decenios, que ha introducido muchísimos objetos nuevos en demanda de nombre propio, y con ellos también nuevos comportamientos humanos, que requieren ser adecuadamente designados o descritos. [. . .]
>
> . . . entiendo que la lengua española, ni más ni menos que el resto de las lenguas, está sometida hoy, como consecuencia de los profundos cambios experimentados en los últimos tiempos por la sociedad, a una intensísima transformación, con adaptaciones prácticas imprescindibles y, por su urgencia, precipitadas, que, en algún que otro aspecto, adaptaciones tales pueden suponer sin duda una pérdida de calidad con renuncia a sutilezas y complejidades expresivas, pero que, en cuanto exigencia funcional, muestran cómo la sociedad a cuyo servicio se encuentra el idioma no yace, arrinconada al margen de la historia, sino vive en la plena actualidad.

■■ What do you see as the challenges to the development (and even survival) of languages nowadays, including some of those referred to here by Francisco Ayala?

Ayala ends his article on a positive note, expressing faith in the future of Spanish. This is a sentiment clearly shared by other custodians of the Spanish language, such as in the following article.

LOS DIRECTORES DE ACADEMIAS RESALTAN EL AUGE ACTUAL DE LA LENGUA ESPAÑOLA

El Congreso de La Rábida reune a 20 especialistas mundiales . . . 'Nuestro idioma goza de una salud extraordinaria . . . ' asegura . . . el director de la Academia Norteamericana de la Lengua Española.

El español, sin embargo, sufre numerosas amenazas. El mayor peligro proviene de las lenguas de carácter comercial . . . como el inglés . . . 'A veces se ve influído por anglicismos, con ruptura de la sintaxis, sobre todo entre los inmigrantes, pero es una lengua viva, armónica, noble, universal, que se puede utilizar para la fuerza del comercio o para goza del espíritu.'

Nicolás Sánchez Albornoz ha indicado que la etapa expansiva de nuestro idioma constituye una realidad en el mundo . . . El auge del aprendizaje del español afecta a Europa y a Estados Unidos, pero también al Extremo Oriente y a los antiguos países comunistas.

(*El País*, 19.I.94)

Whilst acknowledging the usual fear of the influence of English, we can see from this article that another way in which users of Spanish are growing is through the teaching of Spanish as a second/foreign language. Particularly important in this trend have been the activities of the newly launched network of the Institutos Cervantes.

- What do you think this network of institutes might do? What are its likely aims? Can you think of other organisations set up to spread the teaching and culture of a particular language? Is this another form of language planning?

But is there a price to pay for this '*auge*' of Spanish? Does it entail making the language more accessible to international organisations, and thereby sacrificing individual differences? We have already noted that this is sometimes considered a threat in individual countries in Latin America (in Chapter 2 and Chapter 7). Even between widely spoken world languages this could become the case. The influence of English on the vocabulary and syntax of other languages is frequently mentioned. Another highly symbolic action which enraged many concerned with the health of Spanish and its role as separate identity-marker was the decision in 1994 (once again by the association of Spanish language academies) to remove the '*Ch*' and the '*Ll*' as separate letters in the Spanish alphabet.

- Read the following article:

LAS LETRAS CH Y LL SALEN DEL DICCIONARIO

Ecuador fue el único país que votó en contra de la medida. Panamá, Uruguay y Nicaragua se abstuvieron . . . 'A partir de ahora los diccionarios de las Academias no contarán con la che y la elle. Se vuelve al orden romano universal', manifestó el nuevo secretario de la Asociación [de las Academias de la Lengua Española].

Según un reciente informe presentado a la Comisión de la Unión Europea, 'una lengua que no adopte todos sus recursos a un sistema universal y que no facilite su traducción automática se convertirá en una lengua de segunda dentro de la UE'. Este ha sido uno de los principales argumentos de los responsables de esta institución.

Durante las discusiones, esta postura española provocó una réplica muy dura de la representante cubana en el congreso ... 'Estoy a favor de esta medida porque significa que los diccionarios se podrán manejar con más facilidad. Pero también se esgrimieron argumentos relacionados con la Unión Europea que no se deben introducir. Nuestras decisiones son de orden científico y nada más', aseguró Campuzano.

(*El País*, 24.IV.94)

■   Find examples in this article of corpus and status planning.

■   Are you convinced that the eradication of these two separate letters from the dictionary will make an enormous difference to the ease of communication, improve translation services, and so on, as is claimed? Can you think of other motives for pushing for the change?

■■ One particularly significant aspect of this debate and decision is the fact that the initial pressure and suggestion came from the European Union. This supra-national organisation is playing an important role, as we have already seen, in language policies and language behaviours. The Cuban representative at the congress was particularly annoyed by the source of this pressure. Do you think the unity of Spanish may ultimately be threatened by the different European and American political agendas?

It is important to note in this context, however, that similar pressures from the European Union to discard the Ñ, largely with the argument that it presented problems for computer use, were rejected by the Spanish-speaking world. In fact, so proud of this particularly Spanish letter are they that it has been chosen as the logo for the Instituto Cervantes.

It is fitting to end this chapter with an article from the Spanish press, 'Little Ear of the Little Deaf', where the full dilemma of promoting bilingualism in minority languages as part of people's sense of identity versus the utility of using English, with Spanish somewhere in the middle, is satirically presented.

■   Is this the most likely fate for Spanish, and many other languages?

LITTLE EAR OF THE LITTLE DEAF

Joseph Denier

Pauper Oikos llega a su tierra natal, Orejilla del Sordete, un pueblo que rechaza la independencia, pero quiere hacer lo que le venga en gana.

PAUPER Oikos, héroe de los economistas, arribó a la frontera de Orejilla del Sordete, con el objeto de averiguar por qué los nativos querían seguir siendo españoles. Se encontró con un guardia civil, ataviado a la usanza típica y con expresión de agente turístico. Oikos decidió efectuar el saludo europeo en orejillense:

–¡Marescuseta frandraclira smé smé!

–Good morning– respondió el otro, cordial.

–¿Qué ha dicho?– preguntó el economista, estupefacto.

–I said good morning.

–Vd. debe estar borracho– protestó Oikos.

–I'm as sober as a judge– aclaró el guardia –at least, as the judges were before the Ledesma/Múgica mess.

–¿Pero esto no es Orejilla del Sordete?

–This was Orejilla del Sordete– respondió el guardia –and now we are also Little Ear of the Little Deaf.

–Le hablo en orejillense o en español y me responde en inglés. Pauper Oikos frunció el entrecejo.

–¿Entiende lo que digo?

–Yes.

–¿Y por qué no habla orejillense, nuestra lengua madre?– se enfadó Oikos.

–We still use the language at home, together with Spanish, as usual– explicó el nativo –but it would have been stupid to try to impose such an impossible dialect on others.

–¡Pero la autodeterminación!– clamó Oikos.

–Our people– arguyó el guardia –want to be Orejillenses and Spaniards, as always.

–Pero eso no comporta la pérdida del idioma, raíz de nuestra nacionalidad– enfatizó el héroe de los economistas.

–Come on– sonrió el otro –our worries have nothing to do with all that chitchat. Of course we use our language. With it and with Spanish we have two treasures. But with English we have three. Look at Finland, a small country with an incomprehensible language. What do the Finns do? Everyone knows English! So we speak English with the tourists!

–¡Pero yo soy de aquí!

–Sorry, I was just exercising my English.

–Eso es imperialismo lingüístico– se quejó Oikos.

–It's practical, not idelogical!– explicó el otro –if we were living in the tenth century we would have chosen Latin.

–Sois tontos, el español se habla en una veintena de países– se jactó Oikos.

–And what about English?

–¡Pero no tenéis viabilidad económica!

–Who told you that?– ironizó el guardia –we do the same as everybody else in Spain. We pretend that we are poor and we collect money from the FEDER.

Pauper Oikos, imbuido de la polémica de la autodeterminación, no terminaba de comprender qué estaba pasando en Orejilla del Sordete, o Little Ear of the Little Deaf. Fue incapaz de percibir que los orejillenses habían resuelto felizmente el problema de las nacionalidades. Por fin, giró sobre sus talones y se fue. Pero antes se despidió del guardia en orejillense, con el viejo saludo instaurado por Felipe González para reemplazar el adiós.

–Amí– le dijo.

–Bye, bye– respondió el otro, con sonrisa europea.

(*España Económica*, Marzo 1990)

Further reading

On Spanish in the USA and the 'English Only' campaigns, see Fishman (1989; 1991); Bergen (1990); the relevant section of Klee and Ramón-García (1991); and the special edition of the *International Journal of the Sociology of Language*, (number 84: 1991), edited by Florian Coulmas, dedicated to this subject. On Puerto Rico, see Vélez and Schweers (1993). On the spread of world languages, and particularly the dominance of English, see Phillipson (1992).

• • •

Bibliography

Academia Venezolana (1986) *El español y los medios de comuni-cación*, Caracas: Colección Logos.

Alvar López, M. (1986) *Hombre, etnia, estado: actitudes lingüís-ticas en Hispanoamérica*, Madrid: Gredos.

Appel, R. and Muysken, P. (1987) *Language Contact and Bilingualism*, London: Edward Arnold.

Archer, D. and Costello, P. (1990) *Literacy and Power: the Latin American Battleground*, London: Earthscan.

Barros, M.C. (1995) 'The Missionary Presence in Literacy Campaigns in the Indigenous Languages of Latin America', *International Journal of Educational Development* 15: 3, pp. 277–289.

Bastardas, A. and Boix, E. (eds) (1994) *¿Un estado. Una Lengua? La organización política de la diversidad lingüística*, Barcelona: Octaedro.

Batchelor, R.E. and Pountain, C.J. (1992) *Using Spanish: a Guide to Contemporary Usage*, Cambridge: Cambridge University Press.

BBC (1979) *Realidades de España*, London: BBC.

—— (1990) *México Vivo*, London: BBC.

Bergen, J.J. (ed.) (1990) *Spanish in the United States: Sociolinguistic Issues*, Washington D.C.: Georgetown University Press.

Bethell, L. (ed.) (1995) *The Cambridge History of Latin America*, Cambridge: Cambridge University Press.

Boyle, C (1993) 'Touching the Air: the Cultural Force of Women in Chile', in Radcliffe, S. and Westwood, S. (eds) *'Viva' Women and Popular Protest in Latin America*, London and New York: Routledge.

Bull, T. and Swan, T. (issue eds) (1992) *Language, Sex, and Society*, issue no. 94 of *International Journal of the Sociology of Language*.

Burke, P. and Porter, R. (eds) (1987) *The Social History of Language*, Cambridge: Cambridge University Press.

Butt, J. and Benjamin, C. (1988) *A New Reference Grammar of Modern Spanish*, London: Edward Arnold.

Carr, R. (1966, 1982 2nd edn) *Spain 1808–1975*, Oxford: Oxford University Press.

Cebrián, J.L. (1980) *La prensa y la calle*, Madrid: Nuestra Cultura.

Cebrián Abellán, A. (1992) *Marginalidad de la población gitana española*, Murcia: Universidad de Murcia.

Centro de Investigaciones Sociológicas (CIS) (1994) *Conocimiento y uso de las lenguas de España*, Madrid: CIS.

Chiodi, F. (ed.) (1990) *La Educación indígena en América Latina*, vols I and II, Quito: P.EBI(MEC-GTZ) and ABYA-YALA/Santiago, Chile: UNESCO/ OREALC.

Cooper, R. (1989) *Language Planning and Social Change*, Cambridge: Cambridge University Press.

Coulmas, F. (issue ed.) (1990) *Spanish in the USA: New Quandaries and Prospects*, issue no. 84 of *International Journal of the Sociology of Language*.

—— (ed.) (1991) *A Language Policy for the European Community: Prospects and Quandaries*, Berlin and New York: Mouton de Gruyter.

Crowley, T. (1989) *The Politics of Discourse: the Standard Language Question in British Cultural Debates*, London: Macmillan.

Crystal, D. (1987) *The Cambridge Encyclopedia of Language*, Cambridge: Cambridge University Press.

Díaz Cintas, J. (1995) 'El subtitulado como técnica docente', *Vida Hispánica* 12, pp. 10–15.

Díez, M., Morales, F. and Sabín, A. (1977, 1980) *Las lenguas de España*, Madrid: Ministerio de Educación.

Edwards, J. (1985) *Language, Society and Identity*, Oxford: Blackwell.

—— (1994) *Multilingualism*, London and New York: Routledge.

Fasold, R. (1984) *The Sociolinguistics of Society*, Oxford: Blackwell.

Fishman, J. (1989) *Language and Ethnicity in Minority Sociolinguistic Perspective*, Clevedon: Multilingual Matters.

—— (1991) *Reversing Language Shift*, Clevedon: Multilingual Matters.

Fowler, R. (1991) *Language in the News: Discourse and Ideology in the Press*, London and New York: Routledge.

García Meseguer, A. (1994, 2nd edn) *¿Es sexista la lengua española? Una investigación sobre el género gramatical*, Barcelona and Buenos Aires: Paidós.

Gleich, U. von (1989) *Educación primaria bilingüe intercultural en América Latina*, Eschborn: GTZ.

Grillo, R.D. (1989) *Dominant Languages: Language and Hierarchy in Britain and France*, Cambridge: Cambridge University Press.

Hamel, R.E. (1994a) 'Indigenous Education in Latin America: Policies and Legal Frameworks', in Skutnabb-Kangas and Phillipson (eds), pp. 271–287.

—— (1994b) 'Linguistic Rights for Amerindian Peoples in Latin America', in Skutnabb-Kangas and Phillipson (eds), pp. 289–303.

Hickey, L. (1977) *Usos y estilos del español moderno*, London: Harrap.

Hill, J. (1989) 'Ambivalent Language Attitudes in Modern Nahuatl', in Hamel, R.E., Lastra de Suárez, Y. and Muñoz Cruz, H. (eds), *Sociolingüística latinoamericana*, Mexico: Instituto de Investigaciones Antropológicas de la UNAM, pp. 77–98.

Holmes, J. (1992) *An Introduction to Sociolinguistics*, London and New York: Longman.

Hornberger, N. (1992) 'Literacy in South America', *Annual Review of Applied Linguistics*, 12, pp. 190–215.

—— (1994) 'Language Policy and Planning in South America', *Annual Review of Applied Linguistics* 14, pp. 220–240.

Klee, C.A. (ed.) and Ramón-García, L.A. (assoc. ed.) (1991) *Sociolinguistics of the Spanish-Speaking World: Iberia, Latin America, United States*, Tempe, Arizona: Bilingual Press/Prensa Bilingüe.

Lakoff, R. (1975) *Language and Woman's Place*, New York: Harper and Row.

Lambert, W.E., Hodgson, R., Gardner, R.C. and Fillenbaum, D. (1960) 'Evaluative Reactions to Spoken Language', *Journal of Abnormal and Social Psychology* 67, pp. 617–627.

Lapesa, R. (1980, 8th edn) *Historia de la lengua española*, Madrid: Escelicer.

Lastra, Y. (1992) *Sociolingüística para hispanoamericanos. Una introducción*, Mexico: El Colegio de México.

Linz, J. (1973) 'Early State-Building and Late Peripheral Nationalism against the State: the Case of Spain', in Eisentadt, S.N. and Rokkan, S. (eds) *Building States and Nations*, vol. II, London and Beverly Hills: Sage.

Lipski, J.M. (1991) 'Clandestine Radio Broadcasting as a Sociolinguistic Microcosm', in Klee and Ramón-García (eds).

—— (1994) *Latin American Spanish*, London: Longman.

Lynch, J. (1973) *The Spanish American Revolutions 1808–1826*, London: Weidenfield and Nicolson.

Mar-Molinero, C. (1990) 'Language Policies in Post-Franco Spain', in Clark, R., Fairclough, N., Ivanic, R., McLeod, N., Thomas, J. and Meara, P. (eds) *Language and Power*, London: BAAL/CILT.

—— and Smith, A. (eds) (1996) *Nationalism and the Nation in the Iberian Peninsula*, London and New York: Berg.

—— and Stevenson, P. (1991) 'Language, Geography and Politics: the "Territorial Imperative" Debate in the European Context', *Language Problems and Language Planning* 15: 2, pp. 162–177.

Milroy, L. (1980, 1987 2nd edn) *Language and Social Networks*, Oxford: Blackwell.

Montgomery, M. (1986) *An Introduction to Language and Society*, London and New York: Methuen.

Mühlhäusler, P. (1990) '"Reducing" Pacific Languages to Writings', in Joseph, J.E. and Taylor, T.J. (eds) (1990) *Ideologies of Language*, London and New York: Routledge.

Penny, R. (1991) *A History of the Spanish Language*, Cambridge: Cambridge University Press.

Phillipson, R. (1992) *Linguistic Imperialism*, Oxford: Oxford University Press.

Plaza, P. and Albó, X. (1989) 'Educación bilingüe y planificación lingüística en Bolivia', *International Journal of the Sociology of Language* 77, pp. 69–93.

Radcliffe, S. and Westwood, S. (eds) (1993) *'Viva' Women and Popular Protest in Latin America*, London and New York: Routledge.

Richards, J.B. (1989) 'Mayan Language Planning for Bilingual Education in Guatemala', *International Journal of the Sociology of Language* 77, pp. 93–115.

Romaine, S. (1994) *Language and Society: an Introduction to Sociolinguistics*, Oxford: Oxford University Press.

Ros, M., Cano, H. and Huici, C. (1988) 'Language and Intergroup Perception in Spain', in Gudykanst, W. (ed.) *Language and Ethnic Identity*, Clevedon: Multilingual Matters.

Ryan, E.B. and Giles, H. (eds) (1982) *Attitudes towards Language Variation: Social and Applied Contexts*, London: Edward Arnold.

Salvador, G. (1987) *Lengua española y lenguas de España*, Barcelona: Ariel.

—— (1992) *Política lingüística y sentido común*, Madrid: Istmo.

Sau, V. (1981) *Un diccionario ideológico feminista*, Barcelona: Icaria.

Siguan, M. (ed.) (1980) *La problemática del bilingüismo en el estado español*, Vizcaya: Universidad del País Vasco.

—— (ed.) (1982) *Lenguas y educación en el ámbito del estado español*, Barcelona: Universidad de Barcelona.

—— (1992) *España Plurilingue*, Barcelona: Ariel, translated as *Multilingual Spain* (1993), Amsterdam: Swets and Zeitlinger.

—— (1996) *La Europa de las Lenguas*, Madrid: Alianza.

Skutnabb-Kangas, T. (1981) *Bilingualism or not: the Education of Minorities*, Clevedon: Multilingual Matters.

—— and Phillipson, R. (eds) (1994) *Linguistic Human Rights: Overcoming Linguistic Discrimination*, Berlin and New York: Mouton de Gruyter.

Solé, C.A. (1991) 'El problema de la lengua en Buenos Aires: Independencia o autonomía lingüística', in Klee and Ramón-García (Eds).

Solé, Y.R. (1995) 'Language, Nationalism and Ethnicity in the Americas', *International Journal of the Sociology of Language* 116, pp. 111–137.

Tinsley, T. (1992) 'El lenguaje administrativo: a Case Study in Sociolinguistic Change', *ACIS* 3: 1, pp. 23–30.

Vélez, J.A. and Schweers, C.W. (1993) 'A US Colony at a Linguistic Crossroads: the Decision to make Spanish the Official Language of Puerto Rico', *Language Problems and Language Planning* 17, pp. 117–139.

Wardaugh, R. (1986, 1992 2nd edn) *An Introduction to Sociolinguistics*, Oxford: Blackwell.

—— (1987) *Languages in Competition*, Oxford: Blackwell.

Woolard, K. (1989) *Doubletalk: Bilingualism and the Politics of Ethnicity in Catalonia*, Stanford: University of Stanford Press.

—— (1991) 'Linkages of Language and Ethnic Identity: Changes in Barcelona 1980–1987', in Dow, J.R. (1991) *Language and Ethnicity*, Amsterdam and Philadelphia: John Benjamins.

Zentella, A.C. (1990) 'Returned Migration, Language and Identity: Puerto Rican Bilinguals in dos worlds/two mundos', *International Journal of the Sociology of Language* 84, pp. 81–101

Index of terms

grammatical requirement when two or more forms must correspond.

creole 19
This is a linguistic variety which has developed from a pidgin to become the language of a community.

diglossia 10
This occurs when a speech community employs two linguistic varieties for separate social functions, one considered the 'High' variety and the other the 'Low'.

domain 124
A sociolinguistic abstraction, used particularly when looking at such phenomena as diglossia or multilingualism. A useful explanation of the term is to say that 'a domain involves typical interactions between typical participants in typical settings' (Holmes 1992: 24).

ethnographic 63
A form of research which is the observation of and informal participation in the study of social interactions in natural settings.

hegemony 6
A word which implies predominance of one power (community, state, class, etc.) over another, in the political, cultural and even economic sense.

Hispanidad 16
A term used to encompass all Spanish-speaking communities across the world, with a sense of togetherness resulting from a common past, culture and language.

imperative 76
A grammatical mood to convey commands and instructions.

language
Death (30) can be the result of language contact whereby a minority language is squeezed out by the dominance of a stronger and more widely used language.
Revival (30) describes the situation of a minority and minoritised language increasing its number of speakers, geographic area and linguistic functions, such as Catalan since 1978.
Shift (30) occurs when a speaker or speech community changes to a different language (for example as the result of re-settlement or military defeat).

language planning (LP) 130
This influences or changes in a planned way individual or societal language behaviour.
Acquisition planning (131) is use of the education system by language planners to expand the knowledge of a targeted language.
Corpus planning (131) concerns itself with the corpus of a language, by choosing a standard form and enshrining this in dictionaries, grammars and orthographies.
Status planning (131) seeks to promote a language by enhancing its prestige, in order to make it socially acceptable, widely heard, and the language of culture.

Normalisation (131) is a general LP objective specifically designed to promote minority languages. It seeks to protect a minority language in order that it can fulfil all the linguistic needs of a modern society. Normalisation in Spain seeks to give the minority languages all normal linguistic functions alongside Castilian.

lexical 44
The adjective referring to the vocabulary of a language.

lingua franca 18
A variety chosen for communication between people who do not share the same language.

modal verbs 76
Verbs which express different moods.

morphological 44
The adjective describing word formation.

phonological 44
The adjective which describes the sounds of a language.

pidgin 19
A linguistic variety with a restricted structure and system. It is not a complete language and has no native speakers. It develops from the bringing together of those with different mother tongues, and can ultimately become a Creole.

principle
The **personality principle** (121) refers to the right of an individual person to use their mother tongue wherever they move within a political territory.

The **territoriality principle** (121) enshrines the right of a community to use its mother tongue and to expect anyone else to use it within the boundaries of their particular community.

Received Pronunciation 62
The British accent which has high social prestige and is not linked to any particular region.

Reconquista 4
The long (seven-century) recovery of the Iberian Peninsula from the Moorish invasion, culminating in the reconquest of Granada in 1492.

register 72
The appropriate language for a particular context and linguistic environment.
Field (73) is the appropriate vocabulary or grammatical structure for a given context.
Tenor (73) reflects with appropriate language the relationship being created by a given context.
Mode (73) is the appropriate means of communication for a given context (e.g. spoken or visual).

Renaixença 33 and *Rexordimento* 38
Both are translations (in Catalan and Galician respectively) of 'Renaissance'. They describe movements which flourished in the nineteenth century in Catalonia and Galicia with a re-awakening of pride and interest in their national cultures and languages.

Romance language 5

The term for the group of languages which developed from the Latin spoken throughout the Roman Empire. These languages include: French, Spanish, Portuguese, Italian, Romanian, Catalan, Occitan, Sardinian and Rhaetian. As a result of colonialism there are over 500 million Romance language-speakers in the world today.

Romanticism 11

A European-wide movement of the late eighteenth and early nineteenth centuries. Romanticism emphasised the emotional rather than the rational side of human nature. Politically it coincided with the rising regional nationalisms of this period, with its interest in the past, in mythologies, and in the 'national soul'.

social networks 53

The informal networks which enclose normal linguistic interaction, often overlapping and criss-crossing. These networks will influence the way we speak and may be simple or highly complex, depending on the kind of lives we lead.

standard language 6

The prestige variety of language which becomes the institutionalised norm for a society.

standardisation 10

The way in which the standard language is protected by the following processes: **codification** (10), the creation of the standard norms in such prescriptive apparatus as grammar books and orthographies; **elaboration** (10), which ensures that the standard language retains its capacity to perform all linguistic functions by reacting to changing situations with new vocabulary, terminologies, etc.

syntactical 44

The adjective describing structure at the level of the sentence.

unmarked form 104

This occurs when there is an absence of any particular feature to contrast the grammatical form of a word.

vernacular 5

The native language or dialect of a community.